P9-CEQ-293

THE COMFORTABLE PEW

THE
COMFORTABLE
PEW

BY PIERRE BERTON ❧ A CRITICAL
LOOK AT CHRISTIANITY AND THE RELI-
GIOUS ESTABLISHMENT IN THE NEW AGE
❧ WITH A FOREWORD BY THE REVEREND
ERNEST HARRISON ❧ AND A SPECIAL
PREFACE TO THE UNITED STATES EDITION

J. B. LIPPINCOTT COMPANY

Philadelphia   New York

Copyright © 1965 by Pierre Berton
Printed in the United States of America
Library of Congress Catalog Card No. 65–23204
Third Printing

CONTENTS

PREFACE TO THE UNITED STATES EDITION

THIS IS ESSENTIALLY a Canadian book. Even though much of the evidence and example quoted comes from United States sources, it must be remembered that *The Comfortable Pew* was written for Canadian churchgoers from a Canadian point of view. This does not necessarily make it irrelevant. After all, Canada is very much a part of the continent, economically, socially, and spiritually. And my own studies of contemporary criticisms of Protestantism in the United States suggest that some of the situations described herein are not foreign to American churchgoers.

Obviously it is necessary to set the book and its author in the proper context for American readers. For the circumstances under which this short critical analysis was initiated, together with its subsequent publishing history, are unique:

The Comfortable Pew was written at the invitation of the Anglican Church of Canada, which is a child of the established Church of England in Great Britain and a sister to the Episcopal Church of the United States. The author, who is a former Anglican and who now attends no church, was asked to examine the Church as critically as he wished from the viewpoint of an outsider.

The Comfortable Pew was born in controversy and uproar especially within the Anglican Church. The General Board of Religious Education, which conceived the idea, was heavily attacked by various synods and Church bodies across the country. From genesis to publication the clamour was unceasing.

The Comfortable Pew, even before publication date, broke all existing publishing records in Canada. At this writing some 150,000 copies have been printed. No other book in the history of Canadian publishing has approached this record. In Canada a book can sell 3500 copies and make the best seller lists. A sale of 5000 is considered excellent, a sale of 10,000 phenomenal. It is possible to guess that *The Comfortable Pew* may eventually pass the 200,000 mark. Neither the Church, the author nor the publishers expected anything of the sort.

The book had its genesis in the spring of 1963 when the Reverend Ernest Harrison wrote to ask me if I would care to write the Church's Lenten book for 1965. He explained that the Church had had little success with its Lenten books and that it was felt that a "name" writer of stature might produce something both stimulating and critical.

I did not intend to accept the assignment. My interest in the Church was minimal and I was extremely busy. I was heavily involved in a nightly one-hour television program and a regular fortnightly page for *Maclean's*, Canada's largest mass magazine. Yet I was intrigued; I postponed a decision and suggested to Mr. Harrison that he get in touch with me later in the summer.

In the interim my page was unexpectedly dropped from *Maclean's* under circumstances that attracted national notoriety. Because of certain views expressed on the subject of the teen-age sexual revolution, I came under heavy fire from some church groups, including Anglican. (The details of this incident are given in Chapter One, Section Five: "Can Christian Morality Be Pre-packaged?") It did not occur to me that the Church's Board of Religious Education would wish to renew its invitation to me. But Mr. Harrison and his colleagues remained unperturbed, buoyed up, perhaps, by the urgings of the Anglican World Congress, held that summer in Toronto, that the Anglican Church become a "listening church."

When Mr. Harrison and I met again, he urged me to accept the assignment. He had read my pieces in *Maclean's* and also my former daily column in the Toronto *Star*, Canada's largest newspaper. He said he felt I was equipped to do the job the Church wanted: to take an outsider's point of view and say as frankly as I wished what was wrong with it; to sum up the various widespread criticisms of the Church in plain, easily understood language; and to lay the groundwork for a continuing dialogue in which the Church might undergo the painful but necessary process of ruthless self-examination.

I should perhaps say a word here about the Anglican Church in Canada. It is the second largest of the non-Roman Catholic denominations, ministering to some fifteen per cent of the population as compared to the twenty per cent who list affiliation with the larger United Church—a union of Methodists, Congregationalists, and some Presbyterians. Until recently it was known as The Church of England in Canada. The title change is perhaps as much a mark of the new nationalism as it is of the Church's own search for a separate North American identity.

Historically it has been the upper-class church in Canada, even more so, I suspect, than the Episcopal Church in the United States. The tight little oligarchy known as The Family Compact, which ran colonial Canada in the days before nationhood, was thoroughly Church of England. For decades this was the established church in Canada in everything but law; it was the church of the British officer caste, the church of the political in-group, the church of high society. It was not a rural church in the grassroots style of the Methodist Church in the back townships of Upper Canada, but it was certainly the frontier missionary church for those native peoples who were not Roman Catholic. Its clergymen and its bishops tended to be very, very English; most were Canadians by adoption only. Many brought a colonial attitude to the new nation, and some had difficulty in remembering that in Canada theirs was not a state church.

Thus the Church of England generally represented, until recent years, the forces of conservatism in Canada. When flags were to be waved, it was the Anglicans who waved them. When the status quo was threatened, it was the Anglicans who battled mightily to preserve it. In this they offered a sharp contrast to the Methodist Church and its successor, the United Church of Canada.

The Methodist Church, though puritan in its attitude to pleasures of the flesh (it was responsible for those blue laws which, until recently, made Canadian Sundays among the drabbest in the world), had a social conscience that directly affected Canadian politics and Canadian business practices. North America's only socialist party springs from this Methodist background as does Canada's largest department store, Eaton's, which still draws its shades on Sunday but insists on rigorous honesty in both its advertising and its money-back guarantee. The United Church has, as a legacy, been much more in the forefront of social progress than other Canadian churches, and its sermons and actions often seem more forceful and relevant.

Recently, however—or at least this has been my observation— an odd thing seems to have been happening: the Anglicans, or a portion of them, have become much more radical and thus much less respectable than in the past, while the United Church, in some areas at least, seems to have become the status church.

Perhaps the first public evidence of this was seen at the Anglican Congress of 1963, held in Toronto. Here a great many unorthodox things were said and publicized. This was followed by the publication of *The Comfortable Pew*, and there is no doubt that the event of its commissioning drastically changed the Church's image. Indeed, the moderator of the United Church, in a letter to *The Telegram* of Toronto, praising the book, wrote wistfully that he wished his church had thought of it first.*

At the time of the book's conception, however, the Anglicans were understandably cautious. Mr. Harrison and his colleagues on the board made no attempt to publicize the fact that they had asked me to write a book for Lent. But the word leaked out quickly enough, and the news was first published in *The Observer*, the respected national monthly of the United Church. This item was picked up by the daily press, and almost at once an acrimonious argument was launched. It is doubtful if any previous book has caused so much controversy before it was written or even researched.

* Publication of *The Comfortable Pew* was followed several weeks later by a similarly critical book, *Why the Sea Is Boiling Hot*, commissioned by the United Church. Several writers, including myself, were asked to contribute short essays.

A spokesman for the Church quickly announced that I had been chosen to write the book because I was "an outstanding writer and a man of integrity who can be relied upon to take a strong and balanced viewpoint," but many Church people demurred.

The Anglican Diocese of Toronto "protested emphatically" as did the executive committee of the Calgary Diocese and several others. The commissioning of the book was also hotly debated by the provincial synod of Rupert's Land and the Anglican Diocese of Ottawa, but motions of censure were defeated.

For more than a year the letters columns of the Church press were alive with arguments about the book. "I shall not buy it or read it," one correspondent declared. "Pierre Berton will finish us off," another insisted. A third wrote that the controversy would harm the prestige of the Church. Some church papers attacked the proposed book editorially. The Rupert's Land *News* called for "an agonizing reappraisal in the Pierre Berton case," and even after the book was on the press the *Diocesan Times* of Halifax was urging similar action.

Others took a calmer view. "We are neither for nor against Mr. Berton," wrote the *Canadian Churchman*, "because we have not read his book. When it has been published there will be time enough for judgment." The Primate of All Canada, titular head of the Church, made a similar comment: "I don't know if I'll approve it or not. I won't know until I read it," and one letter-writer felt that the Anglicans themselves, by their comments, were providing me with material for the book. "How dare we be so bigoted!" she exclaimed. "Let the book be published, read and studied, and then let us criticize—fairly." With this view, of course, the General Board of Religious Education was in complete agreement.

As a result of this controversy the publication of the book in the third week of January, 1965, was looked forward to both with anticipation and apprehension. But nobody involved in its publication could have forseen the eventual response.

The Church had ordered 7000 copies for its own distribution, and the publishers had printed an additional 9000 copies for the trade. A first printing of 16,000 is very large for Canada. My previous books had never enjoyed a first printing of more than 10,000; generally the top figure was 5000.

Though more optimistic than my publishers, I did not expect a large sale. I had never treated the task as a money-making venture. Indeed, I had agreed to reduced royalties from the publisher and no advance or fee of any kind from the Church, since I did not want to feel obligated financially to the Anglicans. For me, the writing of the book was a kind of spare-time hobby.

Early in January, however, it became apparent that something spectacular was happening. The publishers could not keep up with orders for the book, and additional printings had to be ordered from high-speed offset presses in Winnipeg. Even before publication day an additional 30,000 copies had to be rushed into Toronto by air, so great was the demand. The press had ignored the release dates and were proceeding to review and write news stories about a work that was not available to the public. The booksellers put *The Comfortable Pew* on sale well before publication day. Several national periodicals carried major articles about it. One, which featured the topic on the cover, set a record by selling out in three days.

By February, the whole country was talking and writing about religion. A friend in Regina wrote me that the local paper, which doesn't always review books, had carried no less than *eight* reviews of this one. This was not untypical. Ministers all over the country began to preach sermons on *The Comfortable Pew*. (One preached a total of sixteen sermons on the subject.) Lay groups, women's auxiliaries, and men's church clubs began discussing it. Almost every major radio and television program dealt with it in some way. A national polling organization reported that forty-eight per cent of its sample of respondents intended to read the book. Mail and press clippings arrived by the bushel basket. The phrase "comfortable pew," with many variations ("comfortable view," "comfortable few," "uncomfortable pulpit," etc.), became part of the language.

It became obvious that the simple act of initiating such a book had had a salutary effect on the Church's image in Canada. Indeed, it now seems to me that this *action* was more important than the specific content of the book itself. Even those who disagreed profoundly with its thesis welcomed its publication. This was as true of non-churchmen as it was of committed Christians. "Maybe there's life in the old Church yet," was a typical reaction. No series of sermons, no public gatherings, no national resolutions, no public relations campaign, no amount of lip-service to revolution could have been as effective as the event of inviting public criticism and responding to it with humility.

The book's contents, of course, have been as widely criticized as they have been praised. It was intriguing to me to discover, after publication, that the harshest criticisms did not come from inside the Church at all but from the outside.

Somewhat to my surprise, most of the letters I have had from the clergy themselves—Anglican, United, Baptist, and Presbyterian—have generally praised the book. Reviews by clergymen, too, have been generally more laudatory than reviews by non-churchmen.

Many ministers have written to tell me that the book is a valuable tool for them. "If you have done nothing else than give fresh impetus to the clergy to insist on change, then you have performed a most valuable service to us," one typical letter remarks. "Thank you for the encouragement your book gives us," writes another. "I count myself in with the *many* non-conforming 'young at heart' who desire with all their hearts that the Church be a *force,* not a *form.*"

A healthy self-criticism runs through much of my mail from clerics. A minister's wife reminds me dryly that, though "the Church may look bad from your vantage point, you should see it from ours!" And a pastoral counsellor writes of "the minority within the Church who are calling for a new Reformation and which includes among its members many who would go much farther than you have gone." He adds: "They do not *fear* that the Church may die within the next few decades; they believe that the Church as it is presently structured *must* die if ever it would find its true life again."

A West Coast vicar confesses that the book raised conflicting emotions within him: ". . . all the way from great glee at seeing some of our sacred cows slow-roasted over an open flame to great sadness when I see myself and my brother priests portrayed with such devastation, honesty, and realism. . . . We chafe under the restrictions and limitations imposed on us by our fossilized structure. It is very hard to try to change things from the inside and yet this is where logical change should come from."

There is an echo of this in many letters, such as this one from a small-town minister writing of the religious establishment and the lack of communication between pulpit and pew. He observes that "one of the difficulties that has marked the church's mission over the decades is that so much of what has been discussed and resolved by such bodies as the Lambeth Conference has not sifted through to the parish level. . . . What Lambeth has recommended, local bishops have been slow and even hostile to implement. In our complex society, the church finds herself creating the image of being 'big business.' If the church is to fulfil her mission it is necessary for her to speak boldly against business ethics which are hardly Christian. To do so could mean that some generous contributors would withdraw their support. If this happened perhaps the church would come alive."

Two letters from the wives of Anglican ministers are typical of several which underline the problems of conformity. The first writes:

It's hell when you don't fit into the nice little groove some people have cut for you. The very things you talked about being preached are preached by my husband. So what happens? They leave! My ear has been bent and my heart just about broken by the miserable remarks some of our "nicest" parishioners have made in conversations on the telephone—telling me how my husband's ministry is chasing the parishioners away just because he doesn't sugar-coat the pill. . . . What's the answer, if you don't conform? In my husband's experience you get the squeeze in both directions. He's regarded as an oddball amongst many of his brother clergy, a bit of a sorehead and radical by others, an excuse for leaving the church by a few parishioners and a reason for not attending by many.

The second letter deals with conformity at a higher level:

The Ecclesiastical Caste System is for me one of the most painful. Two years ago—ten years after ordination—my husband had "arrived." A comfortable suburban parish . . . a personable young priest on the way up and getting more frustrated all the time. He knew that if Jesus should suddenly appear and take a look at his work he would see the same thing he saw in the Pharisees, just dandy on the outside, but hollow. . . . I remember the day he took his thoughts to the bishop. It was the lowest point in his life, for the advice he received was: "Son, you're highly thought of around here, but you're in danger of becoming too idealistic. What you have to do is learn how to conform because there are big things ahead for you. . . ." My husband almost left the organized ministry. Instead he said: "Dammit, there has to be something more and I'm going to find it." . . . He certainly isn't "going places" these days. The same parish isn't nearly as comfortable as it used to be and there are faces missing from the congregation, but we're learning how to love and others are learning, too.

I can quote only a smattering of letters from laymen and concerned ex-laymen, but the institutional aspects of the modern Church obviously bother many of them.

A member of a Bible study group writes me that "the yardstick: 'What would Christ do in a particular situation?' has been replaced by the question: 'Would it be good for the church?'" A former Anglican whose family are regular church attendants writes that "the local church bulletin gives great emphasis to fund-raising but I have never seen an article relating to social-moral issues." A former deaconess who has recently left the Church writes that "it was not the theological issues that upset me but the two faces of the church—one for the pulpit and the other for the laity."

A committed Anglican housewife in Edmonton reports that "I find it impossible to sing *We Thank Thee That Thy Church, Unsleeping* . . . for in so many ways the church *is* asleep." Another from Manitoba says that "your willingness to voice so many of those problems which we have feared to voice has upset the complacency of our home to the glorious point of no return."

An eighteen-year-old, newly confirmed in the United Church, writes that "I have come to the conclusion that the agnostics and the atheists care more about what happens to the church than the complacent pew-warmers." And a Baptist minister turned in-

surance salesman, still a faithful churchgoer, sums up the feeling
in many letters when he says that he finds "the pew most uncomfortable thanks to the very thesis you promote. I say to you without any fear of successful contradiction that I have never wit-
nessed so much uneasiness and unrest as exists at the present time.
There is a very great current of unrest with the way the church
is facing a hungry, fighting, bleeding, restless world."

These necessarily brief quotations are fairly typical of those
who have written to praise the book. Not all of my mail has
been favourable, of course; nor have all of the press reviews. It is
interesting to note that the bitterest and most violent attacks
have come from non-clergy and, often, from non-church people.

The burden of these attacks has been that the book says nothing
that is either new or profound—that most of it is old hat and that
college freshmen and adolescents have been saying the same thing
for years. "So what else is new?" several reviewers have asked.
"What's all the fuss about, anyway?" several more have echoed.

Under the book's terms of reference it could scarcely be otherwise. Many of the ideas contained in these pages are old hat to
me, too; I have held them for more than twenty years; after all,
that is why I left the Church a generation ago. To those who
came to similar conclusions twenty years ago the conclusions
reached in this book are certainly not new.

But then the book is not written for freethinkers and is not
addressed to them. It is addressed to those within the Church
who seek to understand the reasons why the Church has been
losing ground over the past decades with people like me. Obviously
the book is not old hat to them or they would not be buying it
in such quantity, reading it with such avidity, and arguing about
it with such vociferousness. Many have written to tell me that I
have put into basic English half-formed thoughts they themselves have held. Others have said that I have simplified arguments which they have had difficulty in understanding.

There is no doubt that in Canada at least the timing of the
book has had a great deal to do with its success. Views which
atheists and agnostics and radicals within the Church itself have
held for some time are now bubbling toward the surface. It may

be that *The Comfortable Pew* has been the kind of catalyst needed for the inevitable chemical reaction.

For to say that certain arguments and viewpoints are not new is not to say that they are invalid. It can be argued that certain critiques ought to be stated and re-stated until something is done to meet them.

A good many clergymen, while welcoming the book, have also echoed the "old hat" criticism. They have pointed out what I have already admitted in my original preface: that many of the criticisms that I quote come from the mouths of committed Christian leaders. They claim that the progressive clergy within the Church have been saying for years what I put into print in 1965.

I am well aware that this is true. But I am also convinced that these words have been the words of a minority within the Church; that, further, the words have failed to filter down to the lay level; that, if there is indeed a revolution simmering within the Church, it is a long way from erupting and the great mass of churchgoing people are scarcely aware of it. The fact that some clergymen really believe that the Church has undergone a revolution merely underlines the points I have to make about the Church's lack of communication with the world and the pulpit's lack of communication with the pew.

Another general criticism of the book, from the clergy's point of view, has been that I have failed to take into account the positive side of the Church. Many ministers have quoted all sorts of exceptions to my various arguments to prove that I am wrong. I am perfectly aware, as I have written at the outset, that such exceptions exist (and I have from time to time indicated in footnotes my awareness of them). My point is that they *are* exceptions. There are all sorts of good things about the Christian Church and most of them are self-evident. On the personal level the Church has made an enormous contribution to the peace of mind of individuals; it has given solace in times of despair and surcease in moments of loneliness. But it was not the purpose of the author as the Church itself conceived his task to write another laudatory tract. My job was to say what I thought was wrong, not what I thought was right.

Again I have been criticized because I have not quoted heavily from the Bible in this book, because I have had little to say about the spiritual side of the Church, because my arguments have been secular ones. But then if the Church wanted a theological critique, it certainly would not have asked an outsider to write one. As a non-churchgoer I can only write about the Church in relation to non-spiritual matters. Further, it ought to be understood that I am not here attacking Christianity but only the institutional mantle that cloaks it.

A more interesting and more sensible criticism has been one made by many clergymen that the title of the book is misleading. I have, they say, really been attacking The Lukewarm Pulpit and not The Comfortable Pew, since the book takes a narrow definition of the word "Church" and much of the criticism seems to be directed at priests rather than laymen.

There is something in this. Certainly the book is aimed at the hierarchy—the clergy and the influential laymen—simply because any broader definition of the word would result in a diffuse target. "The Church is all of the people," several critics have pointed out. This is true enough, in one sense, but if that definition were used the book would become little more than a critique of Christian society as a whole, and that was never the intent of the author or of those who invited his views.

The truth is that, in spite of what the clergy keep saying about the "Church" being all of the people, almost everybody—minister and layman alike—means something much narrower when he uses the phrase in everyday conversation. When a newspaper or a commentator or a clergyman says "the Church," he almost always means the leadership of the Church rather than the entire body of the congregation in Christ.

Nor do I think the clergy can wriggle off the hook by blaming their congregations for the retarded state of the Church today. If the pews are comfortable, it is because the Church's leadership allows them to be. After all, leaders are supposed to lead and ministers to minister; otherwise why have any clergy? Many ministers have written me agreeing with my book but saying they cannot progress because the laity will not allow it. But is this not another way of saying that the clergy are catering to the comfortable pews, giving the people what they want, making sure the boat is not rocked?

There have been, in addition, certain specific criticisms of several of the points raised in these pages. I should like to deal here with the three that have most often been voiced:

1. It has been said that many of my conclusions are impractical, especially those that deal with the use of such devices as closed-circuit television, since such schemes are prohibitively costly.

As long as the Church remains one of the wealthiest institutions in society, I cannot accept this. In my own country the two major non-Roman Catholic churches raised a total of $100,000,000 in 1963, the last year of record. As of that date their total assets in stocks, bonds, bank accounts, real estate, and other investments totalled $1,365,000,000. The Anglican Church of Canada, which made a $1,000,000 killing on a single stock in 1959, owns a major interest in twenty-seven real-estate development companies. As in the United States, this Church property goes untaxed. Several critics have suggested, probably rightly, that I should have made something of this huge investment in the light of certain Biblical dictums. Certainly no one can convince me that some of this money couldn't be spent on improved methods of getting across the Message.*

2. It has been said that I am inconsistent in appearing to argue for a more flexible code in the field of sexual morals and an inflexible code in other fields, such as nuclear war, business ethics, etc.

Of course I have argued for nothing of the sort. In all secular fields the Church's attitude has to be a flexible one; an unchanging code of absolutes has never worked and never can as long as times, conditions, and environments change. What human love dictates in one period and place may be quite different from what it requires in another.

This is equally true of individual actions and human interactions. In suggesting that the Church has, to a very large degree, ignored the industrial and business revolutions (as it has also

* As a direct result of my section on communication one church did inaugurate, in March, television programs in church.

ignored the sexual revolution), I am not suggesting that its ministers can lay down for all time a specific and detailed code of absolute business conduct. This is not to say, however, that they can dismiss the subject. They can, surely, suggest attitudes based on the Christian principle that one should love one's neighbour as one loves oneself; and they can apply these attitudes, parable-fashion, to specific contemporary situations. Exactly the same thing applies in the matter of the sexual revolution.

Since *The Comfortable Pew* was published, it has struck me with renewed force that there are many parallels between the Church's attitude to the two great postwar revolutions: the new industrial revolution brought about by automation and the new sexual revolution.

In both cases, for instance, the Church's knowledge of exactly what is going on is scanty. The implications of what is happening has, I think, escaped most churchmen.

Secondly, and more important, where the Church has done some investigation, it has tended to proceed from previously held positions which it refuses to question seriously, e.g., sexual activity outside the marriage bed is "wrong," "work" is "good" (as in the old hymn "Work, for the Night Is Coming"), idleness and sloth are "bad," etc. Perhaps these attitudes are correct, but, if they are, the Church should know why, and it will not be enough, in the future, to quote the gospels. All such preconceived ideas ought to be ruthlessly questioned and examined as part of the Church's involvement with the New Age.

3. The third major criticism of the book in Canada has been that in many instances I have appeared to attack the Church because it doesn't always share my personal social and political convictions. In the issues I have outlined, it has been argued, there are many honestly opposing points of view.

No doubt this is true (as it also might have been true in the Germany of the Thirties when there were differing points of view regarding the virtues of National Socialism). But the facts seem to be that in several of the areas discussed herein the major churches *have* arrived at certain definite and public conclusions. My point is not that they have made up their minds; it is that they have lagged behind other institutions in society who came to similar conclusions earlier in the century.

One area of social concern which I have not dealt with in the body of this book is the argument over the morality of the death penalty. It will serve to make my point. Though some clergymen still argue that hanging is necessary to the safety of a civilized society, I doubt that any now believe, as many once believed, that seven-year-olds should be strung up for pilfering spoons. In that sense, then, the Church *has* come to a specific and definite conclusion. But it ought to be remembered that the bishops of the established Church in England were among the very last to change their minds on this point, as they have been on the larger issue of total abolition.

Since *The Comfortable Pew* was published, a good many Christian leaders have pointed out to me, rather proudly, that their churches *have* taken stands against the present armament race. This is commendable, but again the resolutions have come very late in the day, at a time when it has become almost fashionable to say such things.

"Ah, well," the churchmen write me, *"this may once have been true; but no longer. You are out of date. The Church has caught up. We are no longer behind the times."* *

Perhaps so. But the question nags: A generation from now will still another writer in another book be able to say that the Church in the Sixties continued to cater to the comfortable pew by ignoring the uncomfortable issues that lay just below the surface?

For many of the causes that I have outlined are already causes that belong essentially to the past. The battles, in effect, have been won, though mopping-up operations continue. Birth control may seem to be lively controversy today, but, in the Protestant world at least, it is no longer an uncomfortable one. Back in 1912 it was uncomfortable, just as the racial issue was uncomfortable in the

---

* Two weeks after my book was published the front pages came alive with the story of one United Church minister in Cornwall, Ontario, who was forced to resign from his parish because his congregation couldn't stomach the topicality of his sermons (on nuclear armament, race, etc.), or his wife's involvement with politics, or his own insistence on giving premarital advice to prospective brides and grooms.

Twenties and Thirties and the nuclear issue uncomfortable in the Forties and Fifties. The Church must continue to speak out and to act on these matters, but it must also try to understand and come to grips with the problems of the future.

And the uncomfortable but significant issues of the Sixties and Seventies may easily be those on which the Church still lags behind: Is free enterprise a good thing? Is our form of democracy a good thing? Is work a good thing? Is sexual abstinence a good thing? And equally important, can the Church continue to condone a social system that allows increasing luxuries to the white world and permits increasing starvation elsewhere? Can it continue to go along passively with an immigration policy that keeps out the underprivileged, the unskilled, the sick, the homeless, the bereft, the coloured, and the unwanted?

There are those who will continue to say, as many critics of *The Comfortable Pew* have already said, that these and similar issues are matters in which the Church should not meddle. As an outsider I can only disagree, and the book that follows is a measure of my disagreement.

P. B.

Kleinburg, Ontario
June, 1965

FOREWORD

THE UNCOMFORTABLE GAMBLE

I WAS ONCE leader of a church study group which decided to discuss the arguments of agnostics and how we should deal with them. One of our members suggested we invite an agnostic to join us. He pointed out that it was comparatively easy to set up agnostic views in our own church parlour, and then decide whether they were valid or not. It would be of more value if we faced the real thing.

The members were surprisingly uneasy, and more than half opposed the suggestion. Its logic, however, was irresistible, and a reluctant group decided to give the idea a try. We invited one of the leading agnostics in town. He accepted, on condition that we would allow him to bring along some of his friends who shared his convictions. We agreed. It was the best series of meetings we ever held. After a miserable introductory session of nervous sparring, we settled down to some real work; and learned that listening was an exercise that hurt nobody.

When the meetings were over, the analysis made by our church members was revealing. A little over half had at first opposed the suggestion; everybody now agreed that it had proved successful. The general consensus (give or take a few individual modifications) was that, as a result of facing some clearly articulated criticism, we had finished with a stronger idea of what the Church was. Without exception, we discovered that there was less difference between a sincere agnostic and ourselves than we had supposed; those we had invited were clearly seen as men of compassion and insight, who could teach us a good deal. "They knew more about the Church," said one member, "than I did. I felt ashamed."

More subtly, those who had originally opposed the invitation realized that they had underestimated their own position, and had been secretly afraid they might be pushed into a corner. They need not have worried. It soon became evident that this was not a boxing match, but a joint effort to find out something of the truth. Pooling our findings with those reported to us by the agnostic and his friends, there was no doubt about the result. Everybody gained.

During the last few years, there has been much talk about the need for the Church to "listen." We have shown a grand talent for lecturing and hectoring; but we seem unwilling to believe that God works through men outside our ranks, who may have much to teach us and a few legitimate challenges to make.

Several ideas are clear. The first is that the twentieth-century Church is strong—perhaps stronger than it ever was in the days of its political power. It need not stand for ever on the defensive. It can look to the outsider for *help*. The second idea is that we can best understand the views of others by inviting them to express theirs under our own roof and with our blessing. We have printed many books in which Christian writers stated the views of outsiders and then proceeded, without difficulty, to rebut them. Why not ask somebody who would express these views directly and confidently, and who would, in doing so, show us those areas where the Church needed to examine its work with great care?

We therefore asked Pierre Berton if he would write such a book for us. We aimed high, because we thought the subject a major one, and there was a chance that Mr. Berton might see it in this light. We had none of the usual attractions to offer. We could advance him no payment for his research and initial work; and our royalties are normally insufficient to cover an author's costs. Yet the Church had been speaking for some years about the essential need for "dialogue" between ourselves and other people, and

the possibilities inherent in such a dialogue might attract a leading writer.

Mr. Berton agreed, and the results appear in the following
pages. You will judge their effect for yourself. But in the opinion
of the Department of Religious Education of the Anglican Church
of Canada, the book does everything we had wished. It sets up
some of the major matters being debated in today's Church. It
states, with superb clarity, points of view that are widespread
both in the not-so-comfortable pew and in the marketplace. Its
tone is charitable and compassionate, and it popularizes much of
the thinking that has characterized leading church thinkers over
the past decade.

Some readers, of course, will see no good in such a book at all,
and others will simply read it to see the Church get its come-
uppance. Our gamble is that there will be a large number of people who fall into neither of these extreme positions. Some will be
members of the Church; some will not. They will, we hope, share
one assumption—that the Church matters. It matters enough to
join, and it matters enough to leave. It is worth criticizing and
it is worth supporting. It is neither an escape nor an outdated
joke.

As far as Anglicans are concerned, we think that parish groups
have been provided with a vast amount of material, and we will
recommend the book strongly for widespread discussion in our
congregations. I cannot say anything for anybody else, but the
outsider will surely learn something of the Church's nature. It
might also occur to him that the Church is faced today with some
severe problems. These concern the whole of society, and the
Church will have to call increasingly for help from those outside.

Our modern situation is neither comfortable nor amusing. As
Mr. Berton points out, we have to consider the possibility that
the Church might cease to function within the next century. He
does not wish this to happen, but thinks that it will if there is no
radical change. My own opinion, that it will not happen, I hold
because there are other roots not dealt with here and—more important—because I believe that the radical reformation has already begun and that this book may be one of its symptoms.

In preparing his book, Mr. Berton has consulted with members of the Anglican Church—parish priests, laymen, theological leaders, and Church House staff—as well as with members of other churches. Those of us who have been concerned in these preparatory discussions have found them an exciting experience.

The book, of course, is not the last word. It is the beginning, we hope, of a wide-ranging dialogue. We are currently preparing a response to *The Comfortable Pew* and, in the true spirit of dialogue, Mr. Berton is taking an active part in its planning.

ERNEST HARRISON

Willowdale, Ontario

PREFACE TO THE CANADIAN EDITION

THIS BOOK would not have been written if the Anglican Church in the summer of 1963 had not asked me to undertake it. At that time the idea of a critique of organized religion was the furthest subject from my mind. In more than a thousand daily newspaper columns and magazine pieces, I had mentioned the church only a handful of times, and usually in passing. Indeed, on those occasions when I was urged by one or other of my readers to either attack or support the Church, I could not get excited over either prospect. But the idea of a major denomination coming to an outside writer and specifically asking him to be as critical as he wished in a book that would be designed and recommended for Lenten reading was so refreshing that I could not ignore it. This alone suggested to me that there was more life in the Church than I had previously thought.

When I accepted the Church's invitation, I asked my Anglican sponsors—and they readily agreed—to widen their terms of reference and allow me to write about all the major Protestant denominations, for it seemed to me that the major denominations are all united, at least in the similarity of the problems they face.

If I have not gone into the matter of church union in this book, it is because I believe that, without realizing it, the major non-Roman Catholic denominations are already unified in at least

one sense: great masses of churchgoers do not differentiate between them theologically.

In an age when people change their churches as easily as they
change their domiciles, choosing often enough the handiest
church in their suburb; in an age when theological differences
between Presbyterians, Anglicans, and United Churchmen cut
very little ice with the mass of the public; in an age when social
position is more important in the choice of one's denomination
than the specifics of liturgy or doctrine, some of the ecumenical
arguments now going on seem to an outsider to be as inconse-
quential as those famous mediæval discussions about angels dancing on a pinhead.

Thus, in examining the churches from a critical point of view,
it is not difficult to lump them together under the single phrase
"the Church." Most of the points raised in this book apply in some
degree to all the major non-Roman Catholic denominations. So
when I say "the Church," I mean the official majority voice and
leadership of the Anglican, United, and Presbyterian Churches
and, to a somewhat lesser but still significant extent, the Lutheran
and Baptist. I use the word "Church," then, in its narrower sense,
and not in the larger one which connotes the entire body of clergy
and congregation.

This book does not attempt to deal to any great extent with the
Roman Catholic Church, though I suspect many Roman Catholics
may find what I have to say interesting and even relevant. Nor is
this book addressed to those hard-core fundamentalist and evangelical churches with whom I have little in common; they belong
to a world apart. Nor is it addressed to those smaller, specialized
sects, which include the Latter Day Saints, Christian Scientists,
and Seventh Day Adventists, whose attitudes and theology are at
a considerable variance from the mainstream of Protestantism.
Nor, for entirely different reasons, is it addressed to the Society of
Friends (Quakers), who so often turn out to be the exception to
the critical statements contained herein.

There are, of course, exceptions in every denomination. Certainly every general statement I make can be contradicted by the
specific examples of dedicated men. That is why, when I talk of

"the Church," I mean its majority attitudes and actions, and not those of the minority within.

I would not pretend that there is much in this book that is new. Most of what I have to say has been said before, in various ways, and often more eloquently, by others. Many of these have been practising Christians and clergymen. I have quoted some of them in the pages that follow. The mental stimulation from meeting them on the printed page or in person has been one of the compensations of preparing this book. Although I approached the task with some trepidation, I found that I was quickly entering into it with enthusiasm. It has been a rewarding and an exhilarating task.

I hope it will be understood that, though this book is a critical one, the criticism of the Church springs out of a general context which is my own belief that Christianity has shaped Western man for the better, and that without Christianity we would be a poorer and less-inspired people. The Western world differs from the Eastern in several ways, not the least of which are our Christian beliefs that all individuals are brothers, that love is the most powerful and most noble of human emotions, and that sacrifice is sometimes necessary for freedom. If the Christian Church is ailing, it is certainly worth reviving; and whether or not it declines and falls, these concepts are part of our heritage. They form the basis of our Western ethics and even of our Western democracy. Every Christian nation has a national conscience that springs directly from the New Testament and which, when aroused, can shape the course of history for the betterment of mankind. It is hard, for instance, to conceive of a Marshall Plan or a Peace Corps emerging from a country that was not inspired, however subconsciously, by Christian principles.

Lewis Mumford, who will be quoted from time to time in these pages, has pointed out in *Faith for Living* that "the Christian belief in the power of love is the very opposite of the barbarian's open love of power";[1] that the Christian capacity for sacrifice— whether it be that of the poet who turns his back on an easy job, a physician who enters a plague-stricken house, or a mother surrendering her private life for the one she brings into the world —is the basis upon which the race survives; and that only those who act on the Christian principle that "he who loses his life shall find it . . ." have the capacity for freedom: for if an individual's life is so dear to him that he will sacrifice anything— betray his friends, renounce the truth, grovel in the dirt—in order to keep his heart pumping and his lungs breathing he is already, for all practical purposes, a slave." [2] Mumford goes on to say that "Christianity accords to all men that equality as whole personalities for which the present political name is democracy." [3]

Mumford, however, also sounds a warning: "Our religion," he says, "should be a repository for the best that has been thought, felt, imagined, divined in each age: but it is rather like a bank that will accept no more deposits because it does not know a safe business in which to invest its capital. Such an institution must presently go bankrupt; one cannot effectively keep the possessions that one has unless one has the courage to put them in circulation and devote them to fresh enterprises and adventures." [4]

In this book I hope to examine some of the areas in which I see the Church going bankrupt. I do not, of course, expect all churchmen or even all non-churchmen to agree with my thesis. It is probably too much to ask anyone to agree with *all* of it. But this book was conceived by the Anglican Church as a catalyst to provoke healthy discussion. If it is to be effective, the points raised here ought to be examined, questioned, and debated. I welcome the debate, as I have welcomed the Church's original invitation. Although there is much about the Church today that I personally find discouraging, one of the several propitious signs is that books like this one can be written, not in the face of Church opposition but under its auspices and even with its blessing.

P. B.

Kleinburg, Ontario
August, 1964

🎵 THE PAST

WHY I LEFT THE ANGLICAN CHURCH

THERE IS an old Anglican hymn of which I am very fond called *"The Day Thou Gavest, Lord, is Ended."* I like it above all others—above, even, the Easter hymns of jubilation and the familiar carols of Christmas—because it takes me back to my childhood Sundays and Evensong in the little Anglican pro-cathedral of St. Paul's in Dawson City. Here, after a summer's day spent picnicking in the blue Yukon hills or drifting on the tawny breast of the restless river, a child could really feel that the gracefully dying day had been a gift to him by an all-wise, all-powerful, and all-embracing deity. Surrounded by family and neighbours, each of whom was an old and intimate friend, listening to the anthems of a choir that included his own mother, insulated by the softly comforting sermons of a man who was a frequent dinner guest, untouched by the dilemmas and perils of that real world beyond the hills, this child could feel at peace with his religion and his God.

For the white-bearded, white-robed God of my childhood was a very real person. Lost momentarily in the mysterious woods behind the town, one babbled almost incoherently to God to keep the bears away. Caught red-handed in some minor childhood crime (such as "talking dirty" or "telling fibs"), one pleaded with God to overlook the sin and keep the gates of Heaven open at least a crack.

I am not sure when this picture of an anthropomorphic God and a finite Heaven began to lose its shape, but I think it probably began on the morning when my Sunday School teacher, an Anglican spinster missionary who worked in the hostel for half-breed children during the week and taught us about Heaven and Hell on Sunday, explained (not without a note of contempt that I should even bring the matter up) that dogs certainly did *not* go to Heaven because they had no souls. I was quite shaken by this revelation: an afterworld that deprived me of my dog seemed to me less than heavenly.

I was more shaken by the three discoveries that followed. First, I learned that Santa Claus, the other supranormal figure in my life, was nothing more than the figment of a pleasant adult conspiracy. Second, I learned that the stork did not bring babies; they were the product of a more interesting process which, by all the evidence it had chosen to give me, my church considered sinful and wicked. The third discovery was even more shattering. For months my Sunday School teachers had been impressing me with the power of prayer. "If you pray hard enough," they had said, "God will answer you." One night I prayed very hard to God to give me and my sister two small, self-propelled automobiles. It never crossed my mind that when I hurried out of the house early the next morning they would not be there. The discovery shook me. And from this point on, I began to be skeptical of everything that was told to me by the adult world in general and by my church in particular.

But I did not reject the Church. God remained a real, if a somewhat less effective, figure. I attended church and Sunday School regularly, though as I grew older I found myself fidgeting through a service grown monotonous with familiarity. In addition, I respected some of the great figures of the church in my town. Chief among these was the Bishop of the Yukon, Isaac O. Stringer, a walking sermon who, in the service of his God and his fellow man, paddled a canoe untold miles, trudged, pack on back, across some of the harshest country known to man, and even on one memorable occasion cooked and ate his boots to stave off starvation. Indians and whites, children and adults respected him for these rugged qualities and loved him for his genuine saintliness.

The second great figure of my middle boyhood was the rector, Mr. Bryne. More than any of the others who came before or followed after, this man devoted himself to the youth of the town. Of all the many clerics whom I was to encounter in my twenty-odd years in the bosom of the Anglican Church, Mr. Bryne was the only one from whom I did not feel, in some sense, remote. He was genuinely interested in boys. He formed us into Cub and Scout groups. He took us on long hikes into the woods, on wiener roasts in the bright summer nights and on week-long camps in the summer. He talked to us frankly about things that counted. Though he never preached, he always had something to say, and when he used parables (as I now realize he did), they were modern ones, based on people and events we all recognized.

The church elders were suspicious and mistrustful of him. For one thing, he was disturbingly cheerful at all times. The comfortable aura of pious sanctity sat ill upon him. The congregation lived in terror that he might commit the unspeakable crime of telling a joke in church, though he never did. Worse, he was an innovator. He wanted to change things around in the service so that the congregation would take a more active part. He wanted some of the boys in the Wolf Cub pack to read the lesson, for instance. This raw radicalism was promptly squashed. Mr. Bryne disturbed people; when it came to the ears of some parents that he had actually discussed the facts of life with the older Scouts, there were shocked whispers. In the end, Mr. Bryne departed and, even to a small boy, the sigh of relief in the adult world was apparent. And, to a small boy, things were never quite the same again without him. Years later I learned that he had left the ministry to become a high-school teacher.

When my family left the Yukon and settled in Victoria, British Columbia (I was twelve at the time), I continued to be a regular churchgoer and Sunday School attendant. My recollections of that particular Sunday School are among the most colourful of my teens. It was simple mayhem. In retrospect, it seems to me that, from the moment I entered the Sunday School hall until the moment I left, I was subjected to a hair-raising barrage of horse chestnuts, B-B's, elastic bands, paper darts, spit balls, gum wads, and the occasional Bible, all of which I returned in kind. There must have been hymns, prayers, and Biblical instructions of a sort, but I cannot recall them. All I can recall is a state of utter anarchy.

After the hurly-burly of Sunday School, the cool church provided a kind of quiet refuge. It was also, for a youth rapidly moving into puberty, a colossal bore. One went because one's parents insisted on it, because the girls in their Sunday best were becoming unaccountably attractive, and because one still harboured the definite belief that, somewhere Up There, a somewhat less anthropomorphic but still-believable God was writing down one's attendance record in a giant ledger against a day of ultimate reckoning. But one did not listen to the prayers, which were babbled by rote, or the lessons, which though beautifully phrased and intoned might as well have been in a foreign tongue, or the sermons, which had nothing to say.

Yet I took my confirmation instruction seriously, examining the sacraments with awe and piety. I remember being genuinely shocked when some of the other boys spoke flippantly of the use of wine in the communion. During this period I was both pious, God-fearing, and fully aware that I was a sinner, probably incapable of salvation. Certain questions nibbled at the fringes of my rationale, but I preferred to put them aside. Where, for instance, did myth end and reality begin? The rector explained that the seven days of Genesis were symbolic—a tale invented for primitive people who could not comprehend modern geological findings. So, too, with Jonah and Noah and the other Biblical figures of the Old Testament. On matters equally miraculous, such as the raising of corpses from the dead and the puzzling business of the virgin birth, he was less explicit. Though something deep down inside me was beginning to ask questions, these questions were never properly formed in my own mind or voiced in class. Nor were they ever answered. We did not think then about the unthinkable.

A few days before my confirmation, I received a baffling house call from the rector. He said he wished to speak to me alone on the eve of this important step. My family withdrew, leaving the two of us shifting about uncomfortably in the dining-room. He engaged in some unimportant small talk, made a few remarks about the seriousness of the move I was making and explained that I could never be the same man again after my confirmation. While I was puzzling over that intelligence, and after one of those awkward little silences that always presages a profound but embarrassing statement, the rector coughed, looked me in the eye, and stated that I should never act with another woman in any manner save that in which I would wish my own sister to be treated. The significance of this remark totally escaped me, and I was left confused and uncertain. Why had the rector travelled all the way to my house and drawn me aside to say that? What was the meaning of it? Did he know I had been fighting with my sister? But didn't everybody? And if I didn't treat other women as I treated my sister, how was I expected to treat them? I could make little sense out of it, but this was obviously the key matter on the rector's mind—that all women should be treated the way I treated my sister. Having said his piece, he took his leave, and shortly after that I joined the church and received, with trembling hands, the chalice of my first communion.

I was a dutiful communicant. Each Sunday I rose before seven, faithfully eschewed breakfast, trudged the mile to church and, a little weak from hunger, took the sacrament. It was never clear to me why I should eat nothing until the bread and wine had passed my lips, or how that kind of denial on the part of a growing and half-famished youth would somehow make him a better man. But I accepted it as part of the Mystery. And it was the Mystery that gripped me in these formative years. Not the words of Christ on the Sea of Galilee; not the moving tales of sacrifice and unselfishness, which had long since lost their meaning through singsong repetition; not even those effectively simple parables, which in another place and at another time had torn at men's souls with all the relevance of a newspaper headline. It was the packaging that intrigued me, not the content; for the packaging obscured the content, or at least that was my experience.

Ritual, alas, cannot long remain exotic when it becomes a

weekly commonplace. It may become as comfortable and as re-
assuring as an old slipper; or it may become a drag. For myself,
and for most of my contemporaries, it became a drag.

Now in the eerie morning silence of the church, broken only
by the low mumblings of the supplicants, I began to listen, for
the first time, out of boredom and curiosity, to what was really
being said: *"We are not worthy so much as to gather up the
crumbs under Thy table."* That sentence had always bothered
me. Most of the businessmen who heard it did not look as if they
would stoop to gather up anybody's crumbs. A few moments
before, the entire congregation had muttered in unison that the
burden of their misdeeds was "intolerable." Was it, really? Or
was this just something that was said because it had been said
a thousand times before, because it was a conventional and even
a comfortable thing to say—a hollow phrase without real meaning? What *were* these misdeeds that were so intolerable?

The ministers in the pulpit talked about wickedness in a vague
way, but I cannot recall that this wickedness was ever linked with
human action, save in the very narrow personal sphere. The grave
injustices and oppressions which were then plaguing the nation,
the inhumanity of man in the mass to man the individual—
matters which were just beginning to concern me at the dawn
of adulthood—were never mentioned. When one entered that
church—or, indeed, most of the other churches that we visited
from time to time—one fled the contemporary world; most of
what was said could just as easily have been said during the
previous century.

Thus began a slow drift away from the Church, unmarked by
any really violent, anti-religious convictions. Mine was a rebellion
born of apathy. More compelling interests entered my life: sum-
mers spent in mining camps, winters spent at college. On the
campus and in the bunkhouse, there were the inevitable religious
discussions. I cannot remember which side I was on.

And then, when I was graduated, I joined the staff of a Vancouver daily newspaper and was appointed, of all things, church
editor. Thus was I exposed almost daily to the Christian Church
in all its curious and disparate manifestations.

From a newspaperman's point of view, the brief contacts I

had with the Roman Catholic clergy were generally the most satisfactory. The Romans did not come pounding on my door asking for publicity; nor did they complain if I got things wrong. But whenever I asked for information or help, they were unfailingly courteous and polite. Only occasionally would their sermons make news.

The Anglicans I found to be snobbish and often testy about giving me help; they felt I should come to church to get information. I tried to explain that I could not attend every service in town, and that by giving me the theme of the sermon in advance for publication on Monday morning, they might widen the circle of their congregation. But I was not always successful. The Anglican sermons were rarely newsworthy anyway.

The United Church people tended to be either very crusty or very eager with the press. Certainly they were worth cultivating, for they often had something to say, at least from a newspaperman's point of view, especially in the fields of drink and morals. If not, they would sometimes ask *me* what they should say, or even make up something on the spot if they thought it would be effective.

The fundamentalists, the evangelists, and the smaller, exotic sects continued to distress me as a human being, just as they intrigued me as a reporter. The most successful leader of all, who attracted the largest congregations and made the most news, told the newspapermen quite frankly (off the record, of course): "I went into this God racket, boys, because I found it was the easiest way to make money."

In my months as church editor, I met a few unselfish and genuinely stimulating men among the clergy, and also a few rogues and charlatans. What really concerned me was the discovery that the vast mass of ecclesiastics differed in no real sense from the vast mass of laymen. They conformed.

Regular contact with the various Christian denominations bred in me a feeling of dismay. Apart from everything else, I was to discover first-hand how hopelessly fragmented the Christian Church appeared to be. The message that was delivered from one pulpit was at odds with the message delivered from another; yet in each instance I was given to understand that this was the only true message—others were false. By this time I was seriously examining the possibility that all were false, for I had rarely seen such a display of mass arrogance on the part of men who proclaimed, always in general terms, their own humility. When I was promoted from church editor, I ceased all church attendance. I had had enough.

In this frame of mind I joined the army and was at once subjected to that peculiar form of military torture, the compulsory church parade. I have often wondered from where the impetus came to make weekly attendance at church compulsory. My experience as a private soldier, a non-commissioned officer, and a commissioned officer suggests that it was compulsory because the weight of the religious establishment insisted that it be so. Certainly the vast majority of the officers and men I trained with considered it a nuisance which they would gladly have dispensed with. From the point of view of the Christian Church, it was surely a disaster.

Simply because it was compulsory, the church parade did more to drive men away from the Church than did any other aspect of the religious establishment. Some men were driven into a white fury by it. I was one. This was because the first chaplain I encountered happened to be a British Israelite who insisted on preaching idiocies to the captive audience that war-time expediency had delivered up to him. Some of us regularly risked detention by arranging for friends to call out our names on parade, while we headed, literally, for the hills.

Here, bathed in the spring sunlight, overlooking the misty Okanagan Valley, we would discuss the whole business of religion. Why did the Church *need* a captive audience, if the message was as exciting as it claimed? After all, in the beginning, the Church did not have to exercise compulsion. Didn't this very compulsion—not only the overt compulsion of the military, but also the subtle compulsion of society—really militate against the Church? Wasn't it possible that by virtue of its various captive audiences the Church in modern society had grown lazy, had ceased to try hard enough to get its message across? And how effective was a Church that seemed to believe it could effectively proselytize men who were dragged unwillingly from their beds and marched, grumbling, to a cavernous drill hall, on the one day the army required no other regular duties? Wasn't the Church kidding itself?

"There are no atheists in the fox-holes," somebody said, with a bitter laugh, and we all joined in the merriment. Of all the nonsense uttered by the pious during World War II, this one sentence was surely the most inane. I did not see a fox-hole during World War II, but those of my friends who did and who entered as atheists also emerged as atheists. The churches offended many of us during the war by subtly encouraging that phrase: it suggested that men could be (and perhaps should be) blackmailed into a form of religion by the imminence of death. No doubt some were, but it has never seemed to me to be a very effective way of getting converts. Dietrich Bonhoeffer, the German Christian martyr who was hanged by the Nazis, and whose influence on modern theological thought has been considerable, shunned this cheap method of boosting religious statistics. Lying flat on his prison floor during a bombing raid, he heard the man next to him, "normally a frivolous sort of chap," mutter the words, "Oh, God, oh, God!" Bonhoeffer wrote to a friend that he could not bring himself to proselytize. "All I did was glance at my watch and say: 'It won't last any more than ten minutes now.' There was nothing premeditated about it; it came quite automatically, though perhaps I had a feeling that it was wrong to force religion down his throat just then." Bonhoeffer added that Christ himself did not try to convert the two thieves on the cross; one of them turned to him.[1]

One Sunday, immediately after my discharge, my mother urged me to accompany her to Matins at the local Anglican church. I went along readily, but when we came out I told her that I could not bring myself to return. We had just come through a long depression and a long war, and the world was topsyturvy. I had been to Europe and back and had seen some of the real problems that distress the human animal. My head was crowded with questions, ideas, vague longings, half-formed resolves, and some small troubles. Whatever it was I was seeking, I did not find it in that church. Instead, I was subjected to a string of religious clichés which, while doubtless comforting to those who seek solace in the repetition of old, familiar phrases, was maddening to me. We were all about to enter a New Age; yet there was nothing in that service to indicate that the world was different, that the language was different, that communication was different, that men were different. Sermon and all, it was a carbon copy of those Sunday rituals in the procathedral in Dawson City in the 1920's.

I was married in the United Church, not for any special reason save that it was my wife's church. It was of little consequence to me who officiated. But when the first child arrived, I had to make some decisions. I felt it proper that my children should be exposed to whatever message the Church had for them, and that they should then make up their own minds, on the basis of this teaching and their own observations, as to whether or not they wished to continue into adulthood as active churchgoers.

Accordingly, I made plans to have my daughter christened an Anglican. In preparation, I read the Anglican order of service for the Publick Baptism of Infants. I found I could not, without hypocrisy, take part in it. The very first phrase that "all men are conceived and born in sin" stuck in my craw, for I simply did not believe it.

First, I do not believe that any new-born baby is either sinful or angelic. She inherits certain characteristics that I would under no circumstances consider sins; apart from that, she is as an empty slate, waiting to be written upon. She may acquire sin, but at the time of christening she is innocent.

Second, and this is perhaps the crux of the matter, I refuse to believe that the act of procreation, which is at once the most sublime and mysterious and ennobling of all acts, can be designated as sinful. This is the clear implication of the passage in the Publick Baptism of Infants. It is also implicit in a good deal of the Church's teachings down through the ages.

Since that experience, a variety of enlightened priests have indicated to me that this passage does not really mean what it seems to mean. I have heard various rationalizations: the Church does not really consider the act of procreation sinful (though it perhaps once did); babies are no longer thought to be inherently wicked (though they once were). All the passage is said to have meant is that we are all imperfect in the sight of God.

Perhaps that is so. But if it *was* so; if that was what the Church

really believed; if the passage that I was required to attest to in
this most sacred moment meant something other than what it
seemed to mean, why—in the name of that God who was being
invoked—why was not all this stated in the clearest possible
English? If the priests of the Church themselves did not believe
the literal truth of what they were saying, why were they required
to say it?

I called a friend in the United Church ministry, who had been
a classmate of my wife and myself at college, and asked him to
go over his order of baptism with me. It was simple, clear, and to
the point. My daughter and the five other children who followed
were baptised members of the United Church.

Twelve years after this incident, the Anglican Church finally
published a revised prayer book. In addition to spelling English
words like "publick" in the modern manner, there were some
other notable changes and omissions. The phrase "conceived and
born in sin" is gone forever. That and certain other significant
events and portents suggest that the Church may be struggling to
make a genuine and honest effort to join the twentieth century,
that, indeed, it may be on the verge of a fundamental revolution
as earth-shaking as the Lutheran Reformation.

But I wonder if that revolution will come in time?

ONE

THE ABDICATION OF LEADERSHIP

1

WAS GOD REALLY ON OUR SIDE?

2

CAN NUCLEAR WAR EVER BE "JUST"?

3

WHAT COLOUR WAS CHRIST?

4

IS GOOD BUSINESS THE CHURCH'S BUSINESS?

5

CAN CHRISTIAN MORALITY BE PRE-PACKAGED?

The Christian churches . . . stand today under God's judgment. Slavery, child labour, the abolition of capital punishment (whether for children committing petty offenses or for murder), economic and social justice, factory reform, religious tolerance, flogging, disarmament, the napalm bomb and the nuclear bomb— all these are matters in which those who have seen have been blinded and often, those who do not see the significance and meaning of the Cross have "seen." For it could hardly be said, for example, that the Bishops of the Church of England have been in the forefront of the battles for reform, reforms which, whether those who have striven for them have seen it or not, are rooted in the assumption that love is more realistically powerful than fear or hate.

From a Sermon on Passion Sunday, 1964, by
Canon John Collins, of St. Paul's, London

1 WAS GOD REALLY ON OUR SIDE?

THE VIRUS that has been weakening the Church for more than a generation is not the virus of anti-religious passion but the very lack of it. Free thinkers no longer rail against religion with the fire of a Robert Ingersoll or the fervour of a Bertrand Russell. Many a sincere churchman today echoes that plaintive cry found in Revelation 3:15: "I would thou wert cold or hot." Large numbers of nominal Christians are no longer either very hot or very cold, for the virus that has weakened the Church is apathy.

The Church to its opponents has become as a straw man, scarcely worth a bullet. "Practically no one expresses any kind of hostility towards religion," wrote the sociologists who studied the British industrial community they called Worktown in 1937 and again in 1960.[1] The typical anti-religious comment was the mild phrase that religion was "a pastime for people who like that sort of thing." [2] The proponents of religion were equally passionless. The most common single reaction in Worktown (actually, Bolton, Lancashire), voiced by more than one-third of the interviewees, went like this: "I approve of religion but don't go to church myself." [3]

Such comments are common on both sides of the water. The man-and-wife team of Robert and Helen Lynd, who made two classic anthropological studies of the American community they called Middletown, found that the openly free-thinking group of the Nineties had been replaced by "an outwardly conforming indifference among a certain minority of the business class." [4] And the sociological summing up of Worktowners' attitudes toward their religion could stand for almost any Canadian suburb: "No real scorn or dislike of religion is openly expressed and very seldom privately. Neither in this series of conversations nor anywhere else did observers come across Worktowners dismissing the whole concept of religion as bunk. . . . There are some who say (nearly always in private) that they would quite like to go to church or chapel but that they feel absolutely bored or appreciably embarrassed by what goes on inside." [5]

If large masses of people are bored with the Church, it is surely because the Church has failed to excite their imaginations or their consciences. And it has failed to do this, it seems to me, because it has had very little to say to them in terms of the twentieth-century world in which they live. Christianity has, in the past, always been at its most vigorous when it has been in a state of tension with the society around it. That is no longer the case. The "divine discontent" that once distinguished the Protestant minister or priest has been replaced by what Mumford calls "a complacent pedestrianism." [6] A great deal of statistical evidence has lately been gathered to demonstrate that most ministers are scarcely distinguishable by their words, opinions, actions, or way of life from the nominal Christians and non-Christians who form the whole of the community.

In the great issues of our time, the voice of the Church, when it has been heard at all, has been weak, tardy, equivocal, and irrelevant. In those basic conflicts that ought to be tormenting every Christian conscience—questions of war and peace, of racial brotherhood, of justice versus revenge, to name three—the Church has trailed far behind the atheists, the agnostics, the free thinkers, the journalists, the scientists, the social workers, and even, on occasion, the politicians. In other areas, the Church has simply stood aloof. It has, for instance, virtually ignored the whole contemporary question of business morals, the tensions within industry and labour, the sexual revolution that has changed the attitudes of the Western world.

In this abdication of leadership, this aloofness from the world, this apathy that breeds apathy, the Church, as Canon Collins stated, has turned its back on its own first principles. No wonder, then, there is indifference.

I have been searching my own mind and memory to discover when the real apathy began. It seems to me, in retrospect, that much of it stems from the wave of disillusionment that followed the misplaced idealism of World War I. For on all sides of this bitterest and most useless of modern conflicts, the Church was in the lead, blessing weapons, waving national banners and announcing that God Was on Our Side. That slogan has since taken on a sour meaning, but there was a time when it was believed implicitly. And it is still believed, though in a somewhat different context and with some changes in phraseology.

The extent to which the Church lined up with the establishment to become, in effect, an arm of the recruiting offices can be discerned in any study of the published sermons of that day. Thus we have the Dean of Durham, Dr. H. Hensley Henson, reporting that "the clergy have almost universally shared the general conviction as to the justice of the moral obligation under which the Nation lies to prosecute it [the war] to a successful conclusion," and that "only through the bitter instrument of fighting can we break the Empire of Force";[7] we have Major-Chaplain A. G. Mackinnon writing that "God . . . is more than a generous Father who benignly smiles on his children. . . . He is a King who leads, who battles, who bleeds with his children";[8] we have the Reverend James Denney, D.D., writing that "we are fighting the battle of truth and humanity, which is the Lord's battle and for that reason can count on his support";[9] and we have Dr. F. Holmes Dudden, Rector of Holy Trinity, St. Austell, and Examining Chaplain to the Bishop of London, preaching that "we are fighting for the triumph of Christ, the salvation of Christendom, the preservation of all that is holiest and best in Christian civilization."[10]

This temptation to invoke God as a political ally, to rationalize the use of force as a Christian instrument, and to equate one's own nation with all that was morally and spiritually decent, was not confined to the British clergy. There is no lack of published comment from American pulpits. We have the Federal Council of Churches of Christ claiming that America was fighting "to vindicate the principles of righteousness";[11] we have the dean of the divinity school at the University of Chicago, Dr. Shailer Matthews, writing that "the cause we fight for is God's cause";[12] we have his opposite number at Yale, Dr. Charles Reynolds Brown, crying that "our cause is just" and suggesting that America is "called of God to be in its own way a Messianic nation in whose mighty unfolding life all nations of earth may be blessed";[13] and we have one minister, the Reverend Abraham Rihbany, announcing that "in such a conflict I cannot think of Christ as being neutral; He stands for us" and urging that "every American mother surrender her son to God and to this great and sacred duty of 'making the world safe for democracy.' " [14]

But if the British and American clergy each felt that their nation was especially chosen of God, so did the German clergy. *Gott Mit Uns* was the cry. "The German soul is God's soul and it shall rule over mankind," said Pastor Lehmann,[15] a comment that was attacked by a Yale professor of practical theology, Henry Hallam Tweedy, as blasphemy, though it was remarkedly similar to the one expressed by his own dean on behalf of the American soul. Pastor Baumgarten approved the sinking of the *Lusitania* "from the bottom of my heart." Said he: "Whoever cannot conquer his sense of the gigantic cruelty to unnumbered victims and give himself up to the honest delight at the victorious exploit of the German defensive power—him we judge to be no true German." [16]

Just as Earl Haig called upon God to be with him when he sacrificed tens of thousands of men for a few yards of Passchendaele clay (and urged at the same time that the chaplains soften up the troops by preaching about Great Britain's objectives in the war),[17] so Hindenburg also appeared to have a direct hot line to the deity. The newspaper *Die Friedenswart* reported in February 1916 that the great general "prepares his plans in collaboration with God. He is in constant communication not only with the different bodies of troops but also with the supreme Arbiter of Battles, with the King of Kings who dwells in the heavens above —this is why God is with him and gives him success." [18] As for the Kaiser, he attributed his victories over Russia directly to "God's hand in history" and went on to say that the "German people has in the Lord of Creation an unconditional and avowed ally on whom it can absolutely rely." [19]

In the reassessment of that terrible and mistaken conflict that followed, it became quite clear that the war was not really fought for those ideals that sent the ordinary man rushing to the colours, usually with the enthusiastic backing of his church. The poets and then the novelists of the Twenties and Thirties, and the historians and pundits of the Fifties and Sixties, have made it apparent that the Great War was fought for petty and silly reasons of national and personal pride at enormous and wholly unnecessary sacrifice; that it could easily have been prevented; and that, after it began, it could probably have been stopped, had Christian charity, Christian good sense, and Christian courage been practised; that no national combatant had Right wholly on his side and that no nation was wholly wrong; that bravery and nobility were shown by members of all armies; and that atrocities, butcheries, and general callousness were by no means confined to any one army, race, or nation.

In the light of recent histories of the war such as *In Flanders Fields,*[20] *The Guns of August,*[21] and *The Price of Glory,*[22] the jingoistic pronouncements of churchmen on all sides sound hollow and even blasphemous, and the general failure of the Church as a whole to act against the war appears disastrous. It is scarcely surprising that the tens of thousands of men who had their ideals shattered in this conflict could no longer make common cause with organized religion; for in its militant pronouncements during World War I, organized religion seemed to have moved a long way from the original Christian principles of humility, forbearance, non-violence, and love. There were some members of the religious establishment who actually contended that these principles would not work in time of war. The echo of that argument is still heard in the nuclear age.

2 CAN NUCLEAR WAR EVER BE "JUST"?

IN WORLD WAR II, the churches were more hesitant about invoking the name of the deity as a kind of national supergeneral, although several of the sermons in *Front Line Religion,* a collection of chaplains' exhortations to the troops, which was published in Britain in the early days of the war, suggest just that: One man talks of "Christian patriots" and speaks approvingly of the Roman army which garrisoned Palestine in St. Paul's day and "kept the peace";[23] later the same chaplain jumps and tramples on Christian philosophy in the same way the Roman jumped and trampled on it in Paul's day, when he preaches, again with approval, on the necessity of shooting sentries who fall asleep on duty;[24] another attempts to argue, fairly incomprehensibly, that "God allows wars *because* He is Love." [25]

The Allied generals continued to find in the Lord a serviceable ally during World War II. Most of them made use of him from time to time. MacArthur, for instance, attributed his first great single victory over the Japanese to "merciful Providence," [26] and Marshall exclaimed that "the hand of the Lord was over us" [27] when American troops first landed in Africa.

The German leaders, having discovered in the previous conflict that God was *not,* apparently, on their side after all, had long since deposed him in favour of Wotan. With one or two memorable exceptions, the German churches, like the Pope, failed to speak out against Hitler. The Allied churches did not make their voices heard in the immoral and (it now turns out) militarily senseless bombings of open cities, such as Dresden, that culminated in the hideous climaxes of Nagasaki and Hiroshima. It is significant perhaps that the most immoral acts of the war (from an early Christian point of view) were precisely those that did not work out practically. Both saturation bombing and the concept of unconditional surrender, for instance, served only to stiffen the resistance of the enemy and prolong the war.*

I have searched the newspapers following the first published news of the atomic explosions in Japan to try to find evidence that somebody of stature in the Christian Church called out against this national denial of the Christian message. There is very little, and most of what there is *says* very little. The Vatican's immediate comment was confined to a statement denying a published report

---

* As R. H. S. Crossman has pointed out in his study of the mass bombing that brought about the destruction of Dresden, "the most senseless single act of mass murder committed in the whole course of World War II" did not shatter German morale, as hoped—quite the opposite. As a result of Goebbels's skilful exploitation of the disaster, "the German people were convinced that the Anglo-American forces were indeed bent on their destruction. And their morale was once again stiffened by terror of defeat." Dresden was a target, Crossman says, of "negligible military significance." [28]

that it had opposed the use of the bomb in Japan. The Primate of All Canada announced that "history is working out the purpose of God," gave it as his opinion that the bomb would stop war— "thus good is the ultimate result" [29]—and in a later statement he said that everybody needed some religion "that would make sense out of the confusion." [30] Other individual ministers used the news of the bomb to call for a return to religion, but few if any attacked the use of the bomb itself or called for its abandonment as a weapon of war. Nor did any of the major churches.

Undoubtedly Christian consciences were privately troubled. Canon John Collins tells me that he received a letter from Geoffrey Fisher, then the Archbishop of Canterbury, "in which he said that it would absolutely outrage Christian conscience were these bombs to be developed after the war. But, alas, when the time came no such official voice was ever raised in protest, and the Church, as part of the 'Establishment,' has continued to sit on the fence, and so by implication support whatever government has been in power in its policy of nuclear armaments."

Yet no Christian who visits the Peace Memorial Museum in Hiroshima can experience anything less than shame when he realizes that we roasted the Japanese to death over a slow fire as surely as the Nazis tortured the Jews. No Christian, passing by one glass case among the hundreds on display, can do less than weep for the rape of his creed when he reads the inscription in English that accompanies the photographs of a smiling little boy and a heap of small curled objects not easily identifiable: "a junior high school boy of fourteen, working outdoors at Zatoba-Cho, twelve hundred metres from the hypocentre, received severe burns that proved fatal. Shown here with his picture are pieces of finger nail and skin which he tore off in his agony as he struggled in vain for five days and nights before death finally relieved him." Does Christian passivity, in the face of this evidence, really differ from the German pastor's approval of the torpedoing of the *Lusitania*?

In the two decades since Hiroshima, the churches have been slow to make up their minds about the moral implications of nuclear warfare. The leadership of conscience has come not from established Christianity but from scientists, many of whom no longer call themselves Christians.

During most of the nuclear age, the statements issued by the major churches (when they have been issued at all) have been weak and contradictory. There have, of course, been proclamations announcing that all war is evil and modern war especially so; but the churches have not closed the door on that evil. As late as 1963, for instance, the Primate of All Canada was saying that he "did not see how Canadians can condemn a nation possessing a nuclear deterrent provided it is determined *to use it with restraint and to strike only hard enough* to end aggression." (Italics mine.)

The United Church of Canada does not seem to be able to unite behind any single firm conclusion regarding the use or development of nuclear weapons. The recent Moderator, Dr. J. R. Mutchmor, has approved the use of nuclear weapons by Canadian troops in NATO and, though there has been much dissent within the Church, its official publication has backed him up.

The Secretary of the Presbyterian Church's Board of Evangelism, the Reverend A. J. Gowland, declared in 1962 that if war breaks out Canadians should use nothing but "modern" weapons —including nuclear weapons.[31] (As the "Overture" on nuclear weapons to the Eighty-Ninth Assembly in 1963 made clear, there are two apparently irreconcilable points of view on the subject within the Presbyterian Church of Canada, one holding that "the possession of nuclear weapons by at least some of the nations of the free world is justified," the other opposing the whole idea of a "balance of terror" as incompatible with Christian morality). These "any means to an end" statements sound strange coming from Christian lips.

There are, of course, many *political* arguments for the manufacture, testing, and possible employment of nuclear weapons; but political arguments are not necessarily Christian arguments. It is odd to find the physicists and biologists who edit *The Bulletin of the Atomic Scientists,* many of them non-believers, protesting against the manufacture and deployment of nuclear arms on the basis of Christian ethics and morality, while the devout journalists who edit or write for *The United Church Observer* sometimes take a different view on the basis of national expediency.

J. Milton Yinger, the sociologist and anthropologist, who has discussed the sociology of regligion in his book *Religion, Society and the Individual,* believes the enormity of the holocaust that would result from a nuclear war, rather than inciting the churches to intense effort, would partially paralyse them. Though Christianity is supposed to be a universal religion transcending national boundaries, in Yinger's tentative view "the churches of America have done very little to confront the average layman in the local situation with a universalist critique of the policies of government during [the cold war]." [32]

The questions that the Church ought to be asking itself in this context are these:

Can any Christian in good conscience support the mass killing of civilians as a means to an end?

Can the Christian Church count itself part of any ruling establishment that condones this?

Does the doctrine of "massive retaliation" fall in with Christian concepts?

Is expediency ever a proper motive for a committed Christian?

Since the time of St. Augustine, the Christian Church, in which pacifism was initially a dominant idea, has lived with the concept of "the just and mournful war"—a war that the Church supports if the cause of one side is manifestly just and if the war is fought without vindictiveness. It was this concept that allowed the clergy in the two great world wars (not to mention the more abortive Crimean and Boer Wars) to utter a call to the colours. The unrestricted bombings and unconditional surrender terms of World War II seem to me to have made mincemeat of the "just war" argument, but it continues to be used in the nuclear age and is fairly obviously the basis of recent statement about deterrents and defence made by the Anglican Primate and the United Church Moderator. The argument for nuclear war is the same argument that was used in previous "just wars"—to wit, it can be condoned by Christians if its cause is moral, if the gains to be made are greater than the losses which appear likely, and if the warfare is conducted with "restraint" so that efforts are made not to endanger non-combatants. This is pretty well the position of the World Council of Churches, whose pronouncement in 1964 on

the subject of disarmament was, in a memorable comment by
Associated Press, "mild and calculated not to offend"—a phrase
that might be taken as a slogan for the religious establishment in
the age of the Bomb.

It is perhaps time that the Church began to reassess the arguments for a "just war" in the light of twentieth-century scientific
advancement. We have, after all, moved some distance from the
pikepoles of the Augustinian era.

When—as all combatants are now agreed—victory is impossible,
when weapons have become so devastating that both sides can be
destroyed, can *any* modern war be justified?

Is the near extinction of an entire nation or the human race
justified under any circumstances?

How can anyone continue to talk about "restraint" or "non-
combatants," when the weapons have become so powerful that
they can wipe out a city or poison the skies for several hundred
miles around?

What is moral or Christian about the preparations for a war
that can make the air unbreathable and the world unlivable?

The Church, in short, must ask itself questions based on the
world as it is and not as it was. The Church must join the New
Age.

At the moment, many of the most militant crusaders in the
New Age are those who make no common cause with the Church.
Not long ago a young Canadian named Peter Light, a member of
the Committee for Non-Violent Action, took part in a Peace Walk
from Vancouver to Berlin. Its purpose was to demonstrate passively, in favour of disarmament. It is significant that the movement in which Mr. Light is so passionately involved is deeply
rooted in the Christian tradition, and that its philosophy and
techniques stem from the example of Jesus by way of Gandhi. It
is also perhaps significant that Peter Light is an atheist, as are
many of his confrères.

When crossing Canada during the Peace Walk, Mr. Light and
his fellow walkers, who were all without funds (again in the
Christian tradition), usually stayed in church basements as guests
of local United Church ministers. Here they were given Christian
hospitality, but only occasionally Christian support.

"We got the feeling," Mr. Light explained to me, "that the attitudes of the clergy did not really differ significantly from those of the general population. About ten per cent were for us, ten per cent against us and the rest just apathetic."

When they argued the merits and disadvantages of nuclear disarmament, the Peace Marchers were surprised to discover that the ministers' arguments were political rather than Christian.

"They'd say things like: 'But how can we give away our bombs with the Russian menace hanging over us?' Their questions were so standard—so like the questions of the politicians and the businessmen, that I felt like saying: 'Hey! You're a minister. What about your religion? What about the moral issue?' Sometimes, in the heat of an argument, they would say, almost as an aside: 'Of course, *as a minister,* I would naturally have to be concerned.' But the point is they weren't thinking as ministers; and they weren't concerned."

These casual observations are borne out more scientifically by a poll of American Protestant clergy, which was taken in 1963 by The Fellowship of Reconciliation, with the help of Harvard University. The poll revealed that, as in past years, the bulk of the clergy tended to go along with the majority feeling in the United States at any given time; that, as in past wars, they supported the military program and considered the "Christian" approach inappropriate to deal with the clash between communism and Western civilization. This seems to me tantamount to an admission that Christ's suffering on the cross was a failure.

The pollsters, who used modern sampling methods, discovered that the average Protestant minister, although he believes war is contrary to the will of God, would accept military service if drafted, would rather be "dead than Red," and does not feel the nuclear crisis to be the most important problem of our time.[33] This identification of the clergy with majority feeling on the contentious matters of Christian conscience squares with similar surveys taken in other fields—the racial problem, for instance.

It is only fair to say that there has always been a small band of Christian pacifists whose attitudes are quite different. The most totally committed men in the Canadian Nuclear Disarmament movement are not Unitarians, Jews, or even Quakers, but Angli-

can and United Church ministers, according to Rabbi Abraham
Feinberg, for some years the leader of that movement.

"The trouble is," the Rabbi says, "that these men are rare.
They aren't bishops; they're too committed to become bishops.
They're inclined to be the least respectable in the social sense.
They make people uncomfortable." Rabbi Feinberg (who is by
no means an objective witness) adds that a good many of the
Christian clergy who are not involved feel guilty about it. "They
say to me, 'We *can't* get involved. We have no one behind us.'"

The Rabbi has stated publicly that "Canadian clergymen of all
faiths—except the Unitarians—in their collective bodies have
shown an astonishing ambivalence and vacillation toward the
moral aspects of nuclear armament and war." [34] Privately he has
put most of the blame on the Anglicans:

"They're extremely conscious of military honour and glory.
They're the quickest to wear uniforms, to become service padres
for posh regiments. They're in part responsible for the indifference and active opposition to us. It's not that they're just not
interested; it's more than that. There's been a determined effort
on the part of the upper hierarchy of the Anglican Church against
the adoption of any resolution that might be interpreted to be in
support of our position."

It is possible to believe that the Rabbi is overstating the case
against the major churches. The fact remains that his experience
with them has led him to that belief. If their faith has not been as
bad as he suggests, their communication has.

In another less controversial area, I myself can bear witness to
the indifference and often sullen opposition of the Church. The
Canadian Peace Research Institute had very little success getting
endorsements, let alone active support, from the major churches.
The Catholic Register and *The United Church Observer* both carried damaging articles about it. Yet this was one project that one
might have expected even the most timid minister to support: a
scientific inquiry by trained scientists into some of the causes of
peace and war. The Institute's Director, Dr. Norman Z. Alcock,
now says he believes the organized Church to be one of the
greatest points of resistance to social change. And Dr. Alcock
was once a Christian.

To this, many committed Christians may ask as, indeed, they have already asked: "But what has this really got to do with the Church? Why should the Church get mixed up in politics? Why should the question of nuclear arms or military service be subject-matter for sermons or for Christian action? These things are better left to the statesmen and the politicians, for they are of the world. The Church's interests are not of this world but of the next."

It seems to me that there are two answers to this question, one pragmatic and one Christian. The practical answer is that if the Church insists on concerning itself (as it has sometimes in the past concerned itself) wholly with the hereafter, then the Church is quite likely to go out of business before the twenty-first century dawns. The Church must get with the world, or it will surely perish.

The Christian answer has already been stated, in an editorial in *The Christian Century:*

> The religious leadership in the Western World has an obligation of conscience. It is to remove the religious sanction for the use of nuclear arms which is implied so long as religious people maintain silence about their use. The manufacture, testing and stockpiling of nuclear weapons proceeds on the assumption that under some circumstances they may be used. Religious people have no right to permit the assumption to stand unchallenged. The use of these weapons would loose indiscriminate destruction on the world and thereby violate the essential human right to life.

The Century then gets down to cases:

> Why have Christian leaders a particular responsibility in this matter? Because the existence of man on earth is at stake. Christians are supposed to know God's purpose for man's existence on earth, to be concerned that God's will be done. The God we know through Christ intends salvation of man; that purpose surely would be defeated by the extermination of man. Christian faith has always taught that self-destruction by an individual is wrong. It surely cannot agree that a course of action which would probably lead to collective suicide can be right.[35]

There is evidence that churchmen, in their heart of hearts, know this. The official pronouncements have become bolder of late, though it must be remarked that since the nuclear test-band agreement it has become somewhat more respectable to be in favour of nuclear disarmament. Canon Collins writes me that at the 1964 Good Friday vigil and procession of the Christan CND (Campaign for Nuclear Disarmament) Group, he had the coopera-tion of a large number of clergy and ministers in central London churches. "I have no hesitation in saying that I do not think we would have got this measure of support five years ago." Again, in Britain, in February 1964, the Church of England finally made an unequivocal pronouncement; its governing body, the Church Assembly, by a large majority, backed a 1963 resolution from the British Council of Churches that opposed nuclear warfare and urged Britain to give up its nuclear deterrent. In this, *its first public stand on the subject,* the Church included an amendment of its own, declaring that "the use of indiscriminate weapons must now be condemned as an affront to the Creator and the denial of the very purpose of creation."

One wonders why it took so long for the Church to come to this conclusion. If nuclear devices were an affront to the Creator in 1964, why not in 1954 or 1945? Why the nineteen-year wait? In this case, as in so many others, the atheists, agnostics, Unitarians, socialists, and scientists were all on record before the major or-ganized Christian community.

3   WHAT COLOUR WAS CHRIST?

IN THAT OTHER MAJOR ISSUE of our time, the racial struggle, there is revealed the same pattern of tardiness, apathy, non-commit-ment, and outright opposition by the Church. In the United States, as Dr. Gunnar Myrdal, the Swedish sociologist, discovered in his monumental treatise on *The American Dilemma,* there has been a long-standing conflict between creed and deed.[36] I think there is little doubt that hundreds of thousands who believe in the Christian brotherhood of man have turned away from the organized Protestant religions because the believers have been sickened and disillusioned by the lack of Protestant action. (The Roman Catholics, whose churches are somewhat less stratified socially, have an appreciably better, though by no means perfect, record in race relations.)

Indeed, the history of the race struggle in the United States has been to a considerable extent the history of the Protestant rapport with the status quo. From the beginning, it was the Church that put its blessing on slavery and sanctioned a caste system that continues to this day. This has paved the way for the system of class structure within the Protestant Church that exists throughout the Western world. It is a negation of that Christian equality before God which the Church preaches.

There are many witnesses to this both within the Church and without. Gordon W. Allport, in his classic sociological study *The Nature of Prejudice,* has reported that "through most of America's history, the Church has been a preserver of status quo in race relations rather than a crusader for improvement." [37] The Church, according to Bishop William Scarlett of the Diocese of Missouri, "has acquiesced in the pattern of segregation." [38] Robert R. Moton, in his book *What the Negro Thinks,* reported that the great majority of white ministers remained "astonishingly aloof" from the racial situation, and that "as a class, white ministers appear to have fewer contacts with Negroes than *any group of their race*." [39] (Italics mine.) Frank S. Loescher in his study of *The Protestant Church and the Negro* goes further. He has written that the Church has taken the lead in contributing to the segregation of Negroes, that in sanctioning all-white congregations it has "probably done the greatest injury to Negro Americans," and that it is in danger of becoming, if it is not already, "a symbol of the philosophy of white supremacy." [40]

Those harsh words were written in 1948. Since that time a section of the Church has awakened to its weaknesses; but again it has come to this realization woefully late. At the Anglican Congress in 1963, the Reverend Malcolm Boyd charged that the

Christian white power structure was selling to the rest of the world "a false, incomplete, illusory picture of the American racial problem . . . a self-justifying, distorted, self-righteous image of what has controversially come to be called 'the American Way of Life.' " [41] At the same Congress, the Reverend C. E. Crowther reported that in some southern states the Episcopal Church was continuing to operate segregated schools and churches.[42]

It is perhaps charitable to draw a veil over a subsequent incident in Jackson, Mississippi. Here seven white ministers tried to enter a Methodist church with two Negroes and were charged with trespassing and disturbing the peace. Two Methodist bishops, one of whom was black, were forcibly restrained from entering another place of worship. What possible comment can one make when a church bars its own bishops and charges ordained ministers with trespassing on its property?

Here, before the eyes of the world, the Church has been tried on the most fundamental Christian issue and found wanting. The long history of the civil-rights movement shows that not only did the Church fail to act when others were acting, but that it also failed even to preach. Other great institutions within society—the press and the labour movement, to name two—were well ahead of the established Protestant Churches in calling for a change in attitudes and a change in the law. The Churches, when they finally spoke, merely echoed what had already been said.

In a study of fifteen of the largest of the twenty-five denominations represented by the Federal Council of Churches of Christ in America, Frank Loescher has shown that until 1929 the Church scarcely uttered a peep on the question of race relations.[43] Indeed, as Gunnar Myrdal was to discover, preachers and local religious leaders did not even come out against lynching. Quite the contrary: "Methodist and Baptist preachers were active in reviving the Ku Klux Klan after the First World War." [44] Even in the 1930's, the comparatively few resolutions that were broadly endorsed were generally innocuous and vague. Though one or two denominations began to mention lynching as an evil, there was scarcely a word uttered on the more controversial and basic issue of economic discrimination. In that entire decade, the word "segregation" was used only once in official church pronouncements.

It was not until 1946 that any Protestant denomination gave its attention to the matter of restrictive covenants in real estate. Yet this problem had been on the "must" list of the National Association for the Advancement of Colored People since 1937. One can scarcely quarrel with Governor Eugene Talmadge of Georgia, who said that the churchmen who attacked him for his racial policies were not worth listening to. "When those ministers are ready to open their churches to Negroes and seat them beside whites I will listen to them," cried the embattled redneck.[45] No greater indictment of the Church's ineffectiveness could have been uttered.

The reasons for the Church's general failure of leadership in the racial crisis are complex. Many of them have to do with the entrenched nature of the Protestant religious establishment, the parish pressures on individual priests and ministers, the social-status aspects of organized religion, and the confusion of militant Christianity with "comfort" and "peace of mind"—matters that will be dealt with later in this book. But some of them have to do with the failure of many Christian ministers, and indeed the failure of large sections of the Christian Church, to understand the relevance of Christian morality to the world around them. In the crisis at Little Rock, according to Campbell and Pettigrew of Harvard, who studied it in detail, some ministers "tacitly consented to a public disassociation of moral criteria from the issue of segregation versus integration." [46] And for most of the others, "the religious and moral dimensions seemed simply not to be relevant. . . ." [47]

That they *are* relevant ought to go without saying, and this incompatibility of Christian preaching and Christian action has been one of the major weapons in the hands of the Church's enemies. It is no accident that those Negroes who are most violently opposed to white supremacy have taken upon themselves the trappings of another religious creed and, in doing so, have discarded the traditional Christian weapon of non-violent resistance. No less a man than Dr. Eugene Carson Blake, the chief administrative officer of the United Presbyterian Church in the United States, has warned that if the Church does not break out of its traditional cultural patterns and stand behind Negro demands, the entire black community may become alienated from Christianity.

In recent years, the tiny minority of clergymen who concerned themselves with the racial question has swelled until today it is probable that those who are in some way opposed to any form of segregation outnumber those who uphold it. In addition, large numbers of clergymen are acting as well as talking, and the ranks of the demonstrators in both the south and the north are speckled and often led by white ministers. The passing of a relatively tough Civil-Rights Bill by the United States Congress in 1964 can be ascribed, in part, to strong, organized church pressure. But again the nagging question has to be asked: Is the Church too late? Can it hope to repair in a few years the damage from two centuries of apathy and opposition? I suspect that it can; but only by massive and sustained action. Whether the religious establishment is capable of this massive and sustained action remains to be seen. For the action must be directed not only at the Negro problem but also at the Puerto Rican problem, the Mexican problem, the Oriental problem, the Indian problem, and finally the white problem—the problem of the caste and class structures that continues to plague most churches in the Western world.

It should be said here that, in some other areas of racial unrest in the world, the Church, or a section of it, has acted with courage and boldness. Certainly the Anglican Church in South Africa cannot today be accused of lack of leadership in the grave situation there. The parent Church in England was less forthright. When the Reverend Michael Scott was deported from South Africa in 1950 for his opposition to the government's apartheid policies, he found he had no overt support in England from the Christian churches. It was left to an "unofficial" body, Christian Action, to offer him a platform to put his case to the people. And when Canon John Collins of St. Paul's dared to preach a sermon in which he condemned racialism in any form, and made passing reference to the apartheid policies of Dr. Malan, Prime Minister of the Union of South Africa, he incurred a storm of protest: "I found myself in those days almost isolated and it was many years before it became comparatively 'respectable' to condemn South African racialist policies."

Canon Collins testifies to the continuing difficulty of getting official action in relation to specific problems dealing with race. In 1963, Christian Action was asked to support Christians in the Sudan campaigning for their minority rights: "They had apparently approached the official British Council of Churches, but it had been impossible for them to back the efforts of an independent body, lest the official position of the Sudan Church, as a member of the World Council of Churches, might be in some way compromised."

In Canada there has seemed to me to be a general feeling, at least among some members of the clergy, that the racial situation elsewhere in the world has nothing to do with them. ("Are you suggesting that *we* take part in Freedom Marches?" one of them asked me.) But the racial crisis has become world-wide, and no Christian can ignore it. We look back today through history's telescope and wonder how it was ever possible for the aristocrats of a past age to live their privileged lives of comfortable isolation without a twinge of conscience, while the faces of the poor were pressing vainly against their windows. Yet some future age will certainly recognize the parallel with our own century, in which the Western white man is the aristocrat, living in the privileged isolation of his own continental mansion, while the faces of the dark-skinned press in upon him, vainly pleading for admission. Sooner or later the poor will have to be allowed entrance to the château, or they will tear it down. In this struggle between the privileged and the poor—the white and the dark—the Church must make its own position clear; and since that position will have a good deal to do with immigration policies which, in this country, conveniently screen out the dark people in favour of the privileged, the stand the Church takes is not likely to be wildly popular.

In Canada we have our own small domestic racial crises. As long as we have Indians, we will probably continue to have conflicts. In the beginning the Church failed the Indian by condoning the mentality that made the reserve system possible. It is this system that has kept the Indian outside the white man's society; and as long as he remains outside that society, the Indian will not be treated as an equal but as a dependant. Generally speaking, he has not been treated as an equal by the churches, which have practised a subconscious segregation against him, just as they have practised a subconscious segregation against any person who wears rough clothing instead of the traditional "Sunday best." In this sense, the Church's attitude, in Canada, to the Indian as a lesser member of society has paralleled its attitude, in the United States, to the Negro. The Indians generally are thought of as God's children rather than as God's creatures, and this paternalistic attitude makes itself felt in the phrase "our Indians" that one hears used from time to time by Anglican bishops. I do not wish here to denigrate the work of the Church on the frontier, especially the Anglican Church; some of the best men the Church has produced have been those who lived among the Indians and helped them. Yet one cannot escape the feeling that the missionary to the Indian, like the missionary to the Polynesian, African, and Asian, has been more of a father than a brother.

A more clear-cut racial crisis occurred in Canada in 1941, when a large number of Canadian-born citizens of Japanese descent were stripped of their rights, plundered of their worldly goods, and herded against their will to detention camps away from the Pacific coastal strip.

There is little on the record to indicate that the churches in British Columbia took a militant stand against this racial bigotry. Their sin was non-commitment, as it was in California, where the churches again remained passive. The churches' stand, when it came, came late and was centred significantly in Ontario and Quebec. This instance of action from a distance squares with the findings of the Harvard investigators who studied the integration crisis at Little Rock and discovered that "the less personally affected are the members of a congregation by the issue, the greater is the freedom of the minister to support desegregation during a crisis period." [48]

It is to the credit of the Church in Canada, however, that some time following the Japanese relocation, its leaders made an effort to do something, especially through the National Inter-Church Advisory Committee in Toronto. They tried to deal ethically with the problem, to prevent further government excesses and to (vainly) prevent the disenfranchisement of Japanese-Canadian citizens. It is a measure of the Church's impotence that, though it probably had some influence in preventing the government from going to further extremes, its efforts met with general failure at the parish level.

Once again it was a case of more talk than action. The "Church-Sponsored Placement Plan for Japanese-Canadian Families," for instance, was an absolute failure. Local pastors and priests in small towns were supposed to ask their congregations to sponsor one Japanese family in their community. Not one church did so. In fact the only reply the Advisory Committee received to its blanket request was from a rural church whose farm congregation declared that if any Japanese were placed in their area they would chase them out.

Again, in 1945, the major Protestant churches protested the government's coercive policy of repatriation. But when the Department of Labour in Ottawa wrote to various congregations for specific assistance, the letters went unanswered.[49]

The Church's general ineffectiveness here can perhaps be understood in the light of a Gallup Poll taken at the time. The country was split pretty evenly on the subject of the Japanese-Canadians. So were the churches and the church groups. There was apparently no appreciable difference between the views of practising Christians and society as a whole.

4   IS GOOD BUSINESS THE CHURCH'S BUSINESS?

Is IT POSSIBLE that this failure to accept responsibility in political matters stems from a long-standing mental compartmentalization that sees no connection between what is said in church on Sunday and what is done at the office on Monday? For centuries the idea has prevailed that religion is a personal matter, concerned with the private and not the public side of life. Just as in the officers' mess it is traditional not to discuss three subjects—religion, politics, and women—so in church it has been traditional not to discuss politics, sex, or business, at least in their specific applications.

The Protestant emphasis on purely personal salvation has brought about a separation of the business community from the religious community and allowed the Christian businessman to think on two levels. The Christian virtues to which he pays lip service on Sunday go unrecognized in the harsh cut-and-thrust of his weekday life.

There was a time when the Church set moral standards for all its flock. This was before the industrial revolution and the growth of the present competitive system of individual enterprise. The authors of a recent book about the place of the layman in the Church, *God's Frozen People,* have pointed out that while the Church could continue to describe the older professions—medicine, teaching, law—in terms of service, the newer occupations of industry and commerce, which came later, were left without behavioural guides.[50] This is why the so-called "professions" noticeably continue to operate under a code of professional ethics that, by tacit agreement, does not apply in the same way to ordinary business ventures.

Indeed, the phrase "It's just good business" is often used to excuse an act or practice that, when examined critically, could scarcely be called Christian. The companion phrase "Sorry, it's just not good business" is also used by businessmen as a valid reason for refusing to act in a Christian manner to their suppliers, customers, competitors, or employees. There is a third phrase, the most hateful phrase of all, and the most un-Christian, which is used to salve the conscience and excuse the most callous acts in the name of an inhuman institution: "Sorry, it's nothing personal." The Christian attitude surely must be that *everything* is personal. But in the business world, in which men are sometimes rejected because of colour, age, or whim, that attitude does not prevail.

The businessman and the politician are measured by the Church not in terms of how they conduct their lives or their businesses but in terms of how often they attend the religious club, how active they are in the parish, and how much money they donate

to various religious causes. In such matters, the Church continues
to look in upon itself and not out upon the world. A large percentage of its members, when they enter its portals, check an
important part of their lives in the cloakroom.

"Historically," says Lewis Mumford, "the Protestant Church
grew up at the moment when the breach between politics, eco-
nomics and morals had fully opened." [51] The captains of industry
no less than the workers were left without a code of behaviour,
so that capitalism divorced from religion became almost a religion
unto itself, and remains so. It has surely not been lost on anyone
that the great sales commandment of the twentieth century is
"Thou *shalt* covet. . . ."

The journalists and the trade unions have been well ahead of
the major Protestant Churches in attempting to outline a course
of conduct based on the Christian heritage. They have been per-
ceptive where the Church has been myopic, bold where the Church
has been timid, specific where the Church has been vague. The
many public exposures of moral misconduct, which go back long
before the days of Lincoln Steffens, Ida Tarbell, and Gustavus
Myers, may be labelled "muckraking," but they have served as
modern parables in a continuing sermon to which organized religion has failed to make its contribution. Some of the greatest of
all were preached by Clarence Darrow, a militant atheist.

There was a time when fire-and-brimstone preachers thought
little of singling out and exposing the private sins of members of
their congregations. But when are the public sins of public men
ever criticized in church? When the NBC television network tried
to line up sponsors for a three-hour documentary program on
racial issues, the normal sponsors who occupied the time slots
available begged off because the subject was "controversial" and
they did not want to offend their customers. This is one of hundreds of similar issues (which range from lending practices to sales
methods) on which the Church, if it wished, could make specific
comment from the point of view of Christian ethics. But the
Church, which was silent on this matter, as on so many allied
matters, can scarcely blame the businessmen in its congregation
for fearing controversy when it fears controversy itself.

I recall once being asked by the United Church to advise on

subject-matter for a series of television documentaries it planned
to produce. The documentaries were to be seen by the widest
audience possible, to break fresh ground and to illustrate Christian
ethics. I outlined a series on business morality and honesty in
everyday life, and the suggestion was accepted with enthusiasm.
Seven years later the series has yet to be made. But scarcely a day
passes when examples are not uncovered—usually by journalists
—of various deceptions in business that are often partially condoned by society. The Church, too, condones such deceptions by
its silence.

Only in very recent times, when trade unionism has become
the real religion of the workingman, has the Protestant Church
begun to awaken to its responsibilities in industry. The Church
has generally ignored the labourer and the industrial worker.*
The comment made by Broadus and George Mitchell, who studied
the industrial revolution in the American South, applies generally
to earlier industrial revolutions in more advanced areas: "The
churches have either had nothing to say on the subjects of low
wages and long hours in the mills, or have distracted attention
from economic wrongs by stressing the calamities of individual
sinfulness." [52]

Traditionally the Church's pose in periods of human exploitation has been to try to teach people to live with their misery
rather than to rise above it. "Christian churches generally have,
for the most part, conformed to the power system of the time
and locality," writes Gunnar Myrdal. "They have favoured a
passive acceptance of one's worldly condition and, indeed, have
seen their main function in providing escape and consolation to
the sufferers. . . . [A] church tends to be more other-worldly the
poorer its members are." [53] Myrdal also discovered that this was
equally true of the Negro churches during most of the period of
black exploitation. Until very recently, few Negro churches were
militant; the sermons rarely dealt with practical problems but, on

---

* As always there have been some remarkable exceptions. Some of the
greatest names in Protestantism—Reinhold Niebuhr and Harry Emerson
Fosdick, to name two—have identified themselves with matters of social
concern, preaching among and working for industrial labourers, and helping
to lay the foundations of the so-called "modernist" movement.

the contrary, were designed specifically to induce a complacent *laissez-faire* attitude to life, to help the Negro "bear his lot."

Now, with such omissions finally comprehended, it is permissible to ask whether the Church does not come to a realization of its responsibilities at a point when all the shouting is over. The problems that workingmen and employers alike are about to face have less and less to do with their conduct during working hours, for those hours will occupy a smaller and smaller part of their lives as the century moves on. The problems of the future are likely to be bound up with leisure time.

Nonetheless, here are some basic questions to which Christian answers must be found. What are the Christian implications of the new industrialization? What are the ethics of automation? Has the Church a new role in the coming age of leisure, and what should that role be? Is work always "good" and leisure always "bad," as some of the old hymns and social clichés suggest? What individual rights are likely to be trampled on as a result of a new kind of electronic machine age? Is it likely or even possible that we are about to be enslaved by machines and, if so, what ought the Christian attitude to be? What new moral dilemmas does the new industrialization pose?

These are only a few of the questions that must be asked about the immediate future. It will not be easy to answer them, let alone ask them, since there is some evidence that churchgoers do not care to hear them discussed. Two recent polls—one by *The United Church Observer* in Canada, the other by the mass-circulation weekend supplement *This Week* in the United States—have shown how unpopular the subject "How Can I Take Religion into My Business Life?" really is. In a list of a dozen suggested sermon topics, it ranked seventh in Canada and last in the United States —far behind such standard soothing syrup as "How Can I Make Prayer More Effective?" and "Happier Families through Religion." [54]

If the Church sees its task to be giving the public what it wants, then it will continue to ignore the ethics and morals of business and industry. But the Christian Church is not a commercial television network. Though it has for centuries seemed to be largely an agency for the comfort of its congregations, it cannot long sur-

vive unless, like its founder, it stirs up the people by making large
numbers of them acutely uncomfortable.

5 CAN CHRISTIAN MORALITY BE PRE-PACKAGED?

THE SEPARATION of the Church from the world, the compartment-
alized Orwellian *doublethink* that so many Christian leaders bring
to contemporary problems, the general feeling that "controversial"
matters should not be discussed—these are never better illustrated
than by the Church's attitude to the sexual revolution which, as
much as the Cold War, distinguishes the New Age. The Church
has generally ignored the sexual revolution and, when not able to
ignore it, has done little more than deplore it or engage in those
stock generalities about right and wrong, sin and forgiveness, that
have sprung so easily and lazily to the tongues of its teachers for
so many generations.

In the matter of the sexual revolution, its origins and its significance, the Church has, quite simply, not kept up. Church leaders
are woefully behind the times, and it is safe to say that large
numbers of them do not know what is happening, or do not believe it when they are told. In my own correspondence file, there
is plenty of evidence of this.

There is also some evidence that the Church hierarchy, or at
least a powerful section of it, does not want discussion of this
subject, and on occasion seeks to stifle or prevent further discussion. This was certainly the attitude of those Church leaders who
attacked *Maclean's* magazine for publishing an article of mine
"It's Time We Stopped Hoaxing the Kids About Sex," which I
had hoped would be the first of several dealing with the sexual
revolution and the problems it poses.[55] There were no further
articles.

I was accused on all sides of "advocating" premarital sexual intercourse among teenagers. Some critics, in fact, used phrases like "unlimited" or "unbridled" premarital sex to describe my attitude. Of course, I advocated nothing of the sort. What I actually said was that society was going to have to accept the fact that premarital sex was not *always* a bad thing, and that while virginity and continence were proper for some, they were not *necessarily* okay for all. I further enraged Church leaders by stating that, while my own daughters were pretty level-headed, if they did happen to become involved in a premarital sexual experience, I didn't really believe it would scar them psychologically or wreck their future marriages. I said further that I would rather have them indulge in a full sexual experience than be condemned to suffer the appalling North American pseudo-sexual practice called "petting," a prime cause of frigidity in married women. I said that if my daughters did get "into trouble," they would not be condemned as sinners by their parents, nor would they be forced into an incompatible marriage for the sake of respectability. I added that I hoped my sons would be wise enough in the ways of the world by the time they got married to make their wives physically content as well as tolerant enough to make their marriages compatible.

For these sentiments I was called—in mail and in print—a libertine with a licentious morality, a sexual pervert, a slug, a dirty evil old man, a pornographer, plus several other phrases that are unprintable. It was interesting to note that the most violent letters attacking me in the name of Christian morality themselves used obscene or profane words and phrases which the Church could scarcely countenance.

A large number of official Church groups condemned me publicly and brought pressure to bear upon the publishers of *Maclean's* and its advertisers. The Qu'Appelle Anglican Women's Auxiliary (one of whose members stated publicly that I should be shot) threatened *Maclean's* with a "concentrated boycott." The Catholic Women's League of Canada, meeting in convention in Banff, was urged to boycott both the magazine and its advertisers because of the "distasteful and objectionable article." The Knights of Columbus Ontario State convention recommended that every member who subscribed to the magazine should cancel his subscription; this group later took credit for my departure from *Maclean's*. The Synod of the Anglican Diocese of Huron was asked to take a stand against me for a "poisonous" article, and a resolution was so drafted. The Diocese of Algoma Synod was moved to call for public book-burnings. Dean F. F. Nock of St. Luke's, Sault Ste. Marie, cried that I had "expounded the virtues of premarital relations." The Baptist Church of Ontario and Quebec attacked me in a resolution as a "Godless, materialistic writer" and said, by inference, that I was glorifying sex and contributing to the breakdown of the moral code. John Thompson, President of the Archdiocesan Council of Parent-Teacher Associations, announced that Berton had "proclaimed to the world the unlimited licence he hoped his sons and daughters would enjoy with teenagers of the opposite sex." There were many others.*

I have not been able to discover that any of the individuals or organizations mentioned above launched any sort of investigation of their own into the causes or effects of the present sexual revolution. Or that any of them came up with any kind of suggestion regarding the problem apart from that implicit in their original pronouncements—that all discussion should be stifled.

Many of the clerics who wrote me tried to pretend that there was no sexual revolutions at all. This certainly supplies the context of those letters which state that the "vast majority" of young people are "highly moral"—meaning, I presume, that they are virgins. Clergymen who believe this simply have their heads in the sand. As August B. Hollingshead, the Yale sociologist, discovered when he studied the adolescents of the typical midwestern community called Elmtown: "The ministers do not know what their young people are thinking or doing, and the young people very carefully preserved this gap between themselves and their ministers." [56] Hollingshead reports there is "a barrier . . .

---

* Not all church groups took this attitude. The day of my dismissal from *Maclean's,* the Reverend Ray Hord, Secretary of the United Church's Board of Evangelism and Social Service, praised me and attacked "business interests and moral prudes" for contributing to the end of the discussion. Both *The United Church Observer* and the Muenster *Prairie Messenger,* a Roman Catholic publication of liberal views, published reasoned articles which were both fair and accurate. A good many ministers wrote me encouraging letters.

between the adolescents active in the churches and the ministers." [57] Young people who participate in taboo activity conceal it from their minister, who "because of his calling and position in the value system is isolated . . . and every effort is made to keep him ignorant of what is actually happening in the adolescent world."

Yet even if such a barrier exists, ministers do not need to be in ignorance of what is happening. The Kinsey figures, though they are now out of date, give a pretty clear indication. A much more recent study by Gael Greene, *Sex and the College Girl*, a well-documented report based on interviews with 614 coeds from more than 102 colleges in all parts of the United States, pictures the 1950's as an age of innocence compared with the present day.[58] Miss Greene charts a complete revolution in moral standards at universities in the past seven years, and she remarks that concepts have changed so radically that she can barely believe she herself was graduated from university only a short time ago. Her findings parallel the conclusions that the National Association of Women's Deans and Counsellors came to in 1964, when they too reported a sexual revolution on the campuses of the United States. The background papers pointed out among other things that the new morality allows sexual permissiveness when affection exists, that is, when "going steady" or with fraternity-pin relationships; that while students still give lip service to the "old morality" they no longer practise it; and that premarital relations had been "democratized" by the social revolution and are now accepted at all social and educational levels—thus doing away with the old double standard and giving girls as much sexual liberty as boys have traditionally enjoyed.

In the midst of this upheaval, the Church's attitude remains inflexible: sex outside the marriage bed is a sin. This general statement allows of no qualification. With the usual exceptions, the Church's approach to the whole intricate and painful problem of the modern sexual revolution stops there. In fact, Church spokesmen are fond of stating (as they have many times stated to me) that there can never be flexibility here; it has been that way from the beginning; it always will be. It is said, quite rightly I think, that the Church cannot change its attitudes simply because it may be the popular thing to do. The Church, as I have been told many times in this context, is not in the business of being popular; it is in the business of being morally right. It is an argument, curiously, that one seems to hear only when the clergy are defending themselves in this one area; one rarely hears it used in discussions on some of the other matters detailed in this chapter. As David L. Edwards, the Editor of the Student Christian Movement Press in London, has put it: "It is curious when people with properly high, even rigid, attitudes to sexual morality do not believe that there are any rules for Christians in war." [59]

Notwithstanding what the clergy believe, the Church's attitudes toward sex *have* changed, and quite radically, as have its attitudes in a number of areas. (After all, we no longer consign heretics to the flames in the belief that we are doing them a personal favour; we do not force those who claim the earth revolves around the sun to recant their dangerous theories; nor do we any longer believe—as the Bishops of the Church of England once believed—that by hanging seven-year-olds for petty theft we protect society from mayhem.) There was an age, for instance, when many of the major Protestants sects believed, as one or two minor ones still do, that dancing, even when it involved something as innocent as a Paul Jones, was indescribably sinful, and that those who practised this lustful relationship would suffer torment for all eternity. This theory is no longer generally held; indeed, in many a church hall on a Friday night, young men and women who have scarcely attained puberty can be observed glued in tight embraces and wriggling to rhythms that would not only have scandalized their forbears but would also have caused them to be driven from the Christian communities of their time.

In our own century, there was a time when kissing was looked upon with equal severity. A Christian woman kissed a man only as a seal to an engagement. Today I think it fair to say that the Church does not frown on kissing as it once did. The question no longer seems to be: "Is it wrong to kiss?" but: "Is it wrong to kiss on my first date?" In fact, in the 1960's, mild "petting," if not condoned, is certainly accepted and overlooked, perhaps because many churchmen do not really understand what adolescents mean when they use that euphemism. Petting, of course, is erotic love play; it is the proper preliminary to the sexual act, and most doctors and psychologists who write books on the subject include it as *part* of the sexual act. It is clearly no longer a social taboo.

There are other specific sexual areas in which the Church has performed a grudging about-face. The entire Protestant Church has now swung behind the campaign to legalize the dissemination of birth-control information and the sale of birth-control devices. There are strong indications that the Roman Catholic Church is being forced into changing its own once-rigid attitudes in this regard as well.

It is pertinent to recall that many of the churches that now whole-heartedly favour the idea of family planning by mechanical methods were once as whole-heartedly against it as the Roman Catholics seem to be. It is equally pertinent to remember that the present acceptance of the rhythm system of birth control by the Roman Catholic Church also represents a considerable shift in attitude, and a relatively recent one; the first reference was made to it by Pius XI in 1930; explicit sanction was given by Pius XII in 1951. It is only in this century that *any* form of birth control has been condoned by any of the major churches.

As usual, in the long, courageous, humane, and eventually successful struggle to free womankind from the cruel notion that the female of the species must be condemned to bear children in an unending procession or be made to face the equally cruel frustration of marital celibacy, it was the free thinkers and not the Church who led the way. Margaret Sanger and Marie Stopes were preaching the gospel of family planning before World War I, but the Anglican Church was still fiercely opposed to the whole idea more than a decade later. It was not until 1930 that the Anglican bishops at the Lambeth Conference paid some tentative and grudging lip service to the principle by stating that, while procreation was the primary end in marriage, birth control methods might be used "where there is a clearly felt moral obligation to avoid parenthood." Even this was hedged in by a qualifying statement that the "primary and obvious" method was complete abstinence. And *that* resolution was by no means unanimous. Clearly, as late as 1930, the bishops were of the opinion that sex should not be fun and that sex should not primarily be love; sex was merely a mechanical method of conceiving children.

It was not until 1958 that the Church, by adopting the Warren Report, at last stated unequivocally its conviction that "to produce children without regard to the consequences is to use procreative power irresponsibly." Again, one may ask, why did it take the Church so long to see what was obvious to Margaret Sanger half a century earlier?

The Anglican Church's attitude on birth control is especially revealing, because it involves a complete 180-degree turn in its philosophy: from absolute opposition, it moved in less than half a century to a position from which it is passing resolutions demanding a change in the law that was, in the beginning, church-inspired. There is little doubt that the Roman Catholics, too, will eventually find a way to come to similar conclusions.

The same change in attitudes will, I suspect, prevail in the matter of abortion, which is now looked upon by the churches as a grave sin, akin to murder. The present laws, again church-inspired, make it technically illegal for a child who has been raped to be aborted. I cannot believe that this callous law, which takes from women the control of their own bodies, will long remain on the statute books without amendment; indeed, I suspect the day will come when some of the major churches will be in the forefront of those groups that insist on an amendment. Again, there will be those who will ask the churches: "Why did you wait so long?"

Sooner or later the churches will have to ask themselves whether in an era of over-population it is proper for a mother's life to be risked for the sake of her unborn child. Whether deformed, defective, crippled, or unwanted children (who, being unwanted, may be psychologically deformed) shall be brought into the world at all. And, of course, whether any innocent human being who has been violated should be made to suffer any further consequences. It may be that, on studying these questions, the Church will come to the conclusion that such individual cases cannot be made subject to inflexible rulings.

In the allied matter of divorce, the Church has tended to place more emphasis on rigid principles than upon human situations. Here again, in many Protestant churches, attitudes have been changing. There is not much doubt in my own mind that the next church to amend its thinking regarding divorce will be the Anglican. At the moment, however, the Anglican Church insists, in effect, that a woman whose husband deserts her forever, or becomes incurably insane, or is jailed for life—that woman, innocent party though she may be, must stand condemned to live out the rest of her days without a legal life's companion. She cannot remarry, even if the church-inspired laws allowed her a divorce for any of these causes, which in most of Canada the laws do not. If this is Christian charity, it is a very odd variety.

The key point here, undoubtedly, is the Church's rigid insistence on chastity. A man or a woman may be divorced, but may not remarry; they must remain continent for the rest of their lives. No allowance is made here for youthful error, human failing, or a variety of other imponderables which, often through no real fault of either partner, make continued existence together unbearable and unwise, even when children are at issue (for to raise children in a loveless atmosphere is surely wrong). There is no room here for Christian forgiveness. The Church does not say: "You have erred; now try again with better partners." The sinners are not allowed to try again; they are condemned by the Church to a life of sexual starvation or, in the Church's eyes, of sin.

Many a clergyman will haggle over that word "condemned." One cannot escape the feeling that, even as late as 1965, the Church believes the celibate state to be the finest to which a man is called. In the minds of many—perhaps even the majority—sex, even in the marital state, is slightly ugly, dirty, and probably sinful.

Certainly there was a time when the entire Christian Church seemed convinced of it. Many of our sexual problems today—including the present morbid interest in the subject that allows it to be exploited commercially—spring directly from the repression of sex by a Church that considered the body essentially wicked, the sublimation of the sex drive positively good, a Church

that managed to suggest that the single state was more pleasing
to God than the marital, and that absolute continence meant certain salvation.

One must hasten to make clear that this is scarcely the present
view of any Christian church. Still, one can hardly blame the
average man for believing something of the sort, since the
churches themselves have been remarkably wary of suggesting
otherwise. It is difficult for the uninstructed layman to untangle
the concept of original sin from the idea that sex is sinful, and a
careful reading of the Adam and Eve myth does little to allay that
suspicion. Indeed, the original sin that we are all supposed to
inherit (a dubious proposition in the light of the undisputed
genetic truth that acquired characteristics are not inherited) is
tied quite obviously in the Bible to sex. When Adam and Eve
sinned, they suddenly realized that they were naked—as though
there is something essentially wrong with nakedness—and they
covered themselves. Why? Because in the eyes of the Church the
human body is somehow sinful. This is the message conveyed by
the opening chapters of Genesis and, again, in the New Testament by the story of the virgin birth in which "purity," even in
marriage, is directly connected with virginity. Until very recently
this message was wholly believed in by the vast body of the
Church, and it is still believed in by some sections of it today. It
is still delivered with precious little denial or amendment to
Sunday School classes in the mid-twentieth century.

It is now perfectly apparent that society as a whole, no matter
what it may pretend, does not act as if it believed any of the
above. It has either rejected the idea of sex as sin or—and this is
of equal concern to the Church—it no longer worries about sin;
it enjoys sinning. If sin is equated with enjoyment in the sexual
field, it is likely to be similarly equated in those other fields that
the Church has generally neglected. Just as large numbers of
Roman Catholics no longer heed their priests on the matter of
birth control, so large numbers of Protestants no longer heed
their pastors on the matter of premarital sex. If it is possible now
to see a day coming when the use of birth-control devices by all
Christians will not be considered a sin, is it also possible to see
a time coming when, under certain circumstances and certain

conditions, sexual relations between unmarried adults may not be considered altogether wicked? The tendency of most church-men will be to give a resounding "No!" to that question. But in view of past experience, they might do well to hesitate and con-sider the matter. Certainly the question ought to be examined in the light of the tremendous technical and social advances that the Christian world has gone through in the sexual area.

Scientific advances have conspired to remove for many people (eventually, I suggest, for all people) two of the major concerns surrounding extra-marital or premarital relations: the fear of pregnancy and the fear of venereal disease. The terror of a finite hell has also disappeared for all but the most entrenched funda-mentalists. (The deans of women in the United States, who were quoted earlier, reported that the traditional dire threats about what happens to "loose" girls had lost their fear-evoking powers.) The Church, then, must be prepared to come up with other valid and logical reasons why strict continence should be observed outside the marriage bed. The old answer, "It is wrong," will no longer be enough for the questing youth of the New Age. Youth will ask: "*Why* is it wrong?" and will want the answer spelled out in convincing detail. The Church may believe that it already has the answers, but a glance at the available evidence should make it obvious that the present answers are convincing fewer and fewer people every year. The Church either needs better answers or it needs better communication—or else it needs to rethink its attitudes. In short, it needs to investigate the sexual revolution in depth.

I find it significant that certain Quakers, in Britain, who have been so far ahead of the other churches in most of the issues men-tioned in this chapter, are almost alone in making this kind of investigation. Although their conclusions, even after two years of study, are generally tentative, they do represent a radical change in Christian thinking. Their pamphlet says:

> If Christianity is a true faith, there can be no ultimate contra-diction between what it demands of us and what in practice works. . . . We have no hesitation in taking every now and then an empirical approach—to ask, for instance . . . whether pre-

marital intercourse is necessarily a bad preparation for marriage, whether to have a variety of sexual partners does in fact weaken intimate relations and destroy a community . . .[60]

Other Christian denominations will not agree with the Quakers and their findings, but they owe it to themselves and to Christian society to look very deeply and thoroughly into the matter, before making snap decisions based on the experience of other centuries.

For society has changed profoundly since the days when the present moral tenets regarding male-female relationships came into force; and that change in the past twenty years has been accelerated. The social architecture of the transformation is fairly familiar: the new status of women, which began with political emancipation and continued in business, industry, and the professions; the development of the automobile and the various changes it brought about, especially in the new freedom, new privacy and the simplification of clothing; the continuing gap in years between the age of puberty and the age when a mature and successful marriage can be contemplated; the use and acceptance of erotic symbolism to stimulate sales and the concomitant equation of sex with popularity, status and success. There is in society today a double level of morality: the one that is stated aloud and the one that is practised in private—an official morality and an unofficial one, an "old" morality and a "new."

The Church itself is party, in a passive way, to this double morality, and therein lies its dilemma. At the moment the Church is saying to its young people (quite accurately, if we examine statistics): "It is foolish for you to rush into marriage, especially in your teens. The chances are relatively high that such a marriage will not work. Wait until you get an education, some maturity, and some experience of the world. Then make a careful selection of your life's partner."

But the Church is also saying: "During this period, however long it is, you must be absolutely celibate. You must abjure all eroticism and sensuality. You may love ethereally, but you must on no account love physically." And it continues to say this in an era when the unchaperoned mingling of the sexes begins at an earlier age than ever before, when erotic stimuli—many of them savagely commercial—have never been more prevalent; when all the confining armour of womanhood has been tossed aside; and when the various old-fashioned barriers against clandestine alliance—financial, social, physical, and geographical—have never been lower.

When the inevitable occurs—and the inevitable occurs more and more frequently as the years go by—the Church then says, in effect: "Quick! Get married before the child is born. Then everything will be all right." Marriage, apparently, sanctifies all, even a hasty and ill-advised one; or so we are led to believe by the evidence of those ministers who more and more frequently report the increasing percentage of pregnant brides who appear before them.*

It is time that the Church began to ask itself some questions about the present inflexibility of its attitude to sexual morality. Some of these questions might be:

Is it *always* in the interests of *every* teenager who gets pregnant —or every adult, for that matter—to get married, simply in order to be "respectable"? Are there conceivably situations in which it would be better for her to bear her child, or even abort it, and not get married to its father? What should society's attitude—and the Church's—be to such women, compared with its attitude toward those who go to the altar pregnant?

Is it *always* foolish to marry at a tender age? Or are there conceivably circumstances in which human happiness and well-being is served by an early marriage? Are premarital sex and extramarital sex *always* wrong? On every occasion is it sinful for every kind of person of every age and circumstance? Or are there, conceivably, for some people at some times, human considerations that makes it permissible and even desirable?

Should *every* adult of *every* age, including those with no hope of marriage, be denied all normal sexual satisfaction? What about a situation in which the men greatly outnumber the women, or vice versa; what morality would the Church prescribe in such

---

* Though some ministers, quite rightly, attempt to dissuade pregnant prospective brides from entering into incompatible alliances, few find it easy to go against the grain of a society that insists on respectability first and compatibility second.

conditions? What has been the experience of other societies in
other ages?

What is the most important thing in marriage—human love or
human breeding? Is the chief purpose of the sexual act *always* to
perpetuate the species, or is it possible that in the human kind it is
an end in itself and (quite apart from procreation) the consum-
mation of love?

Does divorce *never* serve the emotional and spiritual welfare
of parents and children, or are there sometimes special occasions
when love requires divorce? And, if such circumstances exist, is it
invariably wrong for the former partners to seek new ones?

All these questions are really the same question: *Can Christian morality be neatly tied up in the form of pre-packaged
judgments?* Can a code of absolutes, in which certain things are
judged always to be wrong, truly form the basis of a Christian
morality? Was this Christ's intent? Did he really seek a morality
in which inflexible rules of conduct over-rode all compassion for
individual people, in which immutable regulations ran roughshod
over human needs?

Is it possible that there may be occasions in which human love
dictates different actions in different circumstances? Should the
emphasis not be on love rather than on regulations?

If it answers these questions candidly, the Church may come
to the conclusion that the old inelastic morality is just as obsolete
in the New Age as the outmoded concept of the just and mournful
war.

TWO

THE TYRANNY OF THE RELIGIOUS ESTABLISHMENT

1
THE WORSHIP OF NATIONAL CREEDS

2
THE ECCLESIASTICAL CASTE SYSTEM

3
RELIGION VERSUS CHRISTIANITY

4
THE CASTING OUT OF THE OUTCASTS

5
THE COMFORTABLE PEW

Where all are Christians, the situation is this: To call oneself a Christian is the means whereby one secures oneself against all sort of inconveniences and discomforts, and the means whereby one secures worldly goods, comforts, profit, etc. But we make as if nothing had happened, we declaim about believing ("He who knows best, that is our priest"), about confessing Christ before the world, about following him, etc., etc.; and orthodoxy flourishes in the land, no heresy, no schism, orthodoxy everywhere, the orthodoxy which consists in playing the game of Christianity.

Sören Kierkegaard [1]

1 THE WORSHIP OF NATIONAL CREEDS

ONE OF THE MINOR PHENOMENA of the post-war North American continent has been the so-called "religious revival." Statistically it is impressive. Films, books, and articles dealing with religion are such sure-fire successes that the cliché phrase used in a thousand magazine titles "How I . . . Found God" has become a classic joke inside and outside of the trade. Columns of religious advice help to sell newspapers. Millions appear to have been influenced by Norman Vincent Peale, Billy Graham, and Fulton J. Sheen. The Church itself has never been financially stronger. In Canada its property values have passed the one-billion mark, its annual income the one-hundred-million mark. The church-building boom, especially in the suburbs, is easily observable: in metropolitan Toronto, for instance, two hundred new churches have been erected in a decade. The polls reveal that almost everybody—some ninety-four per cent—believes in God, accepts the doctrine of the virgin birth and life after death, and is convinced of the power of prayer. Everybody, in short, is a Christian. Yet, oddly, the great revival is rarely if ever referred to as a "Christian revival." The operative word is "religious."

There is another apparent paradox. Though the Church has never been statistically fatter, its influence appears to be waning. In the words of Dr. T. W. Adorno, the Director of the Institute of Social Research, "Religion does not play such a decisive role within the frame of mind of most people as it once did; only rarely does it seem to account for their social attitudes and opinions." [2] Often, as we have seen, these attitudes and opinions are at cross purposes with the Christian ethic. The very people who say they are religious will also admit, when pressed, that their religion has not greatly influenced them. A *Maclean's* survey in 1961, taken in Guelph, Ontario, showed that while most respondents, Catholic and Protestant, attended church regularly and believed it to be

"the home and refuge of all mankind," only a small percentage
were influenced by it in matters of birth control, sexual behaviour, political decisions, public causes, or business conduct.[3]
Where are the Christians in Christendom? Such was the plaintive question posed one hundred and ten years ago by the Danish
philosopher-theologian, Sören Kierkegaard: "The illusion of a
Christian nation is due doubtless to the power which number
exercises over imagination," he wrote.[4] Those words are as true
today as they were in 1854, and they have been echoed again and
again in British and North American society. Peter Berger, the
Christian sociologist, talks of "the Christian malaise";[5] Karl
Barth, the great German theologian, says simply that "the world
which we confront today is aggressively pagan";[6] both Arnold
Toynbee, the historian, and Thomas Merton, the Trappist monk,
have referred to our age as "the post-Christian era." John A. T.
Robinson, Bishop of Woolwich, declares that the decline in religion has been "one of the most obvious features of our time."[7]
And Lewis Mumford has called the institutionalized forms of religion "a mere husk of habit."[8]

One finds it hard to quarrel with Alasdair MacIntyre's contention that in Britain eighty per cent of the population, "mostly
superstitious to some degree," uses the Church only to celebrate
birth, marriage, death, and Christmas, and that this use or misuse
of the Church "is rooted in a set of vague, half-formed, inconsistent
beliefs."[9]

Again, Orwell's *doublethink* springs to mind. Westerners are
puzzled by the Japanese, who are apparently able to believe in two
religions, Shintoism and Buddhism, at the same time; yet there are
many parallels between the Oriental compartmentalization and
our own. The Japanese are married in Shinto shrines and buried
from Buddhist temples, and almost everybody is, at least nominally, both a Shintoist and a Buddhist. Indeed, in the past it has
been not uncommon for a man to be a Shinto and a Buddhist
priest at the same time. Yet, as Donald Keene, Associate Professor
of Japanese at Columbia University, has pointed out, the two
religions are incompatible. A Buddhist believes in the evilness and
foulness of the present world and the beauty and promise of an
afterlife; the Shintoist believes that the only desirable world is

the present one—everything that follows is evil and foul. The Buddhist is convinced that the universe is eternal; there was no creator; the Shintoist believes that Japan was physically born from gods. As Keene says, the union of the two religions was made possible "only because men can divide their minds and accept contrary things at the same time." [10] One should not be too surprised at such Oriental compartmentalization; it exists just as strongly in the Western world, where millions worship, or pretend to worship, two differing and often incompatible creeds.

If the Church has failed to influence the faithful, it is surely because the leaders of the religious establishment themselves worship at another shrine. The anthropologist J. Milton Yinger, noting that the present "hasty return to the church" seems largely superficial, goes on to point out that "a great deal of the operating faith resides in national creeds." [11] (In Middletown, the Lynds found an "almost complete merging of the two areas of religion and patriotism.")[12] Shintoism has, of course, long been the national creed of Buddhist Japan, just as, in the words of a Western social commentator, Will Herberg, "by every criterion, the American Way of Life is the operative faith of the American people." [13] (It is also the operative faith of the Canadian people, and no amount of maple-leaf waving will change that truth.) The Secretary of the American Home Mission Society, Dr. Jitsuo Morikawa, echoes Herberg: "In the most crucial issues of life, friendship and love, marriage and home, death and burial," he says, "the Christian obeys submissively the dictates of American culture and public opinion rather than the claims of the Christian gospel." [14]

"To join many middle-class churches," Yinger writes in *Religion, Society and the Individual*, "is not sharply different from joining Kiwanis." [15] Vance Packard confirms this in *The Status Seekers*: "Today, the doctrinal meaning of joining a particular church is far less important in the decision than the social or business meaning." [16]

And "success" in business and social terms has all too often been the real gospel of the Church. A successful church is like a successful business. If its membership is growing, its budget growing and its program growing, then it is said to be "progressing." The Church existed for three centuries without the need for

building programs; but a church today without an expensive
edifice is becoming unthinkable in the major denominations.
Since pre-Renaissance times, the spectacle of a costly and ornate
cathedral rising above the most squalid slums has been one of the
continuing and paradoxical images of Christianity. It was Janet
Lacey, Director of Inter-Church Aid and Refugee Service for the
British Council of Churches, who raised this question at the
1963 Anglican Congress in Toronto. She asked, tentatively, if the
Church was sure its priorities were in the right order: "Do we
need new churches? Are there not several half-empty, little-used
buildings of all denominations in one town or diocese?" [17] But a
glance at the parish and diocesan press indicates just how important buildings are in the great Numbers Game, which the religious
establishment plays. They reinforce the belief that things really
are going well with the Church—and, of course, things *are* going
well if you accept the social yardstick of success, and not the
Christian one.

In March 1964 the *Diocesan Times* of Nova Scotia gave front-
page prominence and some gingerly worded applause to a speech
by Canon F. M. French, the priest from Sydney Mines, who said,
among other things, that the church's concerns about "bunfights,
budgets, organizations, and tea drinking with parishioners and
finding new ways to get people into the church and raise contri-
butions" was overshadowing its true work.

A glance at that same issue, and other issues of the same newspaper, makes clear how relevant this priest's remarks are. The
emphasis is all too often on statistics, budgets, social events, and
material gifts:

> . . . The Kingston Guild had a successful year financially, their
> main activities being the annual Tea and Sale and catering for
> wedding receptions. . . . The Parish has gone forward during
> the past year. It has reduced its DBM grant by $250. . . .
> Two polished brass candlesticks were dedicated by the rector
> . . . wrought iron railings provided by the guilds have been
> erected at the church entrance. . . . The annual meeting re-
> ports showed a successful year . . . the Women's Working
> Association Pre-Christmas Tea and Sale brought in $306. . . .
> We welcome our new Diocesan Commissioner [whose] record

in the present parish is outstanding. . . . The Parish annual budget has grown from $35,000 a year to $85,000. . . . During Mr. Meadus' rectorship of Fairview, St. John's has achieved a major goal in the building of a splendid new church with basement hall and adjoining parish hall. . . . The Church's business has become big business. In the last ten years our work has increased tremendously and the volume of business in our office has doubled. . . .

I do not mean to point the finger here at a single church newspaper or a single diocese; the same sort of thing can be found in the parochial press of most major denominations. In his recent study of the religious press in the United States, James Fiss reports that, of the millions of words printed in church newspapers and other publications, most deal with internal matters; few are directed toward world problems or religious suggestions.[18] Any study of diocesan newspapers dramatizes the problems the most idealistic parish priest faces when he is under presure to "succeed."

If he wishes to achieve recognition from the community at large, from the congregation, from his fellow ministers, and from the church hierarchy—and if he wishes to move forward in that hierarchy—the clergyman must be success-motivated. He must bring lustre to the physical look of his church by financing the building of a new one or by refurbishing an old one. To do this he must enlist as many members and as much money as possible. His congregation must grow numerically if not spiritually, and the minister himself must become an organization man. If he can "relate" to people, and not rub them the wrong way with too many awkward questions; if he is good at raising large sums from the more affluent members of the parish—and good at keeping them happy—if he is good at "P.R."; if he "adjusts" to the community and does not come into conflict with it by raising too many abrasive points of Christian conscience; if he can balance a budget, expand facilities, and act as a good executive while developing the relatively innocuous skills of the pulpit—all without stirring up the natives unduly—then he will be counted a success; he will be sought out by better-appointed parishes because of his proven abilities in the Numbers Game; his photograph will appear in the diocesan press with the appropriate statistics below it; and he will be marked for continuing promotion.

This success-motivation is likely to be passed on to members of the congregation as a positive value. As Peter Berger discovered, "The church has hardly lagged behind the business world in urging success upon those who are its members." [19]

In Middletown, the Lynds reported: "There is more subtle church rivalry today than formerly, as financial and social competition, particularly among the business class, have tended to replace earlier doctrinal differences as lines of cleavage." [20] As a result, they discovered that Middletown is building religion in its own image; "there is a tendency to appraise the fruits of religion by the same tangible material measurements which it applies to other activities." [21]

The three social researchers who undertook the study of the Canadian upper-status community they called Crestwood Heights reported that "like a newer and finer house, a new and advanced religion can be a powerful source of reassurance to the Crestwooder that he has escaped his hampering past and can now grasp at a more alluring and dazzling future." [22] And in Jonesville, the typical American city studied by the University of Chicago's W. Lloyd Warner with a team of ten social anthropologists, "Few individuals cling to a particular church because of tradition. For most Protestants, theology plays a minor role in the selection of a church. They go where they find their own kind of people. During their lifetime they may belong to several different churches as a result of mobility up or down or because of moving to a new community where the levels of the churches are different." [23]

This practice of shopping for one's religion on the basis of its usefulness, as one shops for any well-advertised product, tends to weaken religious faith. For if religion is accepted for reasons other than for its claim to absolute truth, then one denies that claim, and religion itself is subconsciously rejected by the very people who seize it so eagerly as a tool to worldly achievement. The phrase "nothing succeeds like success" can hardly be made to apply to the Christian faith.

2   THE ECCLESIASTICAL CASTE SYSTEM

THE NATIONAL CREED of North America involves the worship of status and conformity. "The whole system of getting clergy is actually geared to conformity," a young Anglican priest, who has left parish work, told me recently. "At the beginning, you're shipped to a small rural parish. If you adapt, you're moved to a larger community. If you continue to adapt, you're moved to a metropolitan suburb and maybe eventually you attain a bishopric. The key word is 'adapt.' The fellow who is expected to provide leadership is the fellow who is expected to conform."

The best thing, it seems, that can be said of a clergyman today is that he is a regular guy, "one of the boys," "just like you or me." In spite of the prophetic tradition of the Bible, the Church encourages this attitude. Personal opinions, tendencies to radical criticism, a sense of irony, all distinctive personality traits, it seems, must be submerged so that the minister in no way stands out from or apart from his flock. Not only must his own personal tastes and views be sacrificed to those of the mass denominator, so also must those of his wife and children. The worst things that can be said of a minister today is that he is "different," an agitator, a disturber, an eccentric, an oddball, a radical.

The chains of parish life make it difficult for him to break out and be anything else, since so much of his time is devoted to tea-cup balancing and inoffensive palaver with the natives. The idea that healthy churchgoers must have regular visits from their minister is deeply engrained, and much of the cleric's time is spent making the rounds, like a doctor. Many are so tyrannized by parish duties that they have no time to think. When they cease to think they lose their zeal and their commitment.

Yet the parish continues to be the hub around which the major denominations revolve. Not long ago two young Anglicans, about to be ordained as priests, decided they would like to engage in the kind of priest-worker relationship that has been common in some parts of Europe. They asked to be worker-priests, detached from the parish, operating entirely within industry. But their bishop refused the request. He said he could not ordain them as long as there were parishes without ministers. Similarly two young ministers, newly ordained as Evangelical Brethren, decided they should focus their attention on the "inner city," which has recently become a subject of church concern. They were told that this was impossible because their church was rurally based. They quit the Church to become social workers.

Dr. C. R. Feilding, a former Dean of Trinity College, University of Toronto, who has been completing a thorough study of theological schools in North America, believes the system feeds upon itself. It is his impression, based on various psychological tests of Roman Catholic, Protestant, and Jewish divinity students, that the modal (or average) personality of these students is what is known in the jargon as "passive-dependent." It has been discovered that theological students of a markedly aggressive type are unlikely to succeed. Dr. Feilding believes there are three reasons for this.

First, the whole process by which theological students become what they are tends to select those who have been kept apart from the real world. "They're always at the clerical end of the church and not at the lay end. It starts, really, with the parental remark: 'Wouldn't he make a lovely priest?' And it proceeds from acolyte to choir and so on. He's always 'up front' in the church."

Second, there are the theological schools themselves, whose system of teaching by lecture appeals to the passive-dependent personality. "The professor answers all the questions. If there's open and free discussion, the student gets upset. Once he gets out of the seminary, having been trained in the passive-dependent style of life, he fits in admirably. If he's a young clergyman in the Anglican Church and becomes a curate, he'll succeed as a passive-dependent man. There are too many sad stories about curates with bright ideas who got into trouble with the rector. The curate is expected to do the rector's leg work; the system doesn't operate to produce aggressive clergy."

Third, the system is such that the minister's life is composed entirely of response. "The job is such that the passive-dependent type of personality is needed. The local minister is required to respond instantly to phone calls and other requests, dropping everything if necessary. If he doesn't, he's in trouble with the laymen who run the church. The lay people want a 'dependent' minister. The man who proposes to run his own life will probably clash with this kind of set-up."

The result has been that some of the brightest theological students today do not bother with ordination. They feel they can fulfil the Christian ministry in other fields. If they are ordained, they feel they will cut themselves off from those they really want to work with. Thus the Church must seriously ask itself: Is the parish the most important field of work in the New Age? Is it possible we are wasting our best men or driving them away from the Church because the parish dominates all? Are there other areas, besides the parish, or beyond it, which we ought to be concerned with? And if so, what are these areas, and what is the order of priority in dealing with them?

For the dominance of parish life, with its social club atmosphere, means that the church is tightly tied to the secular social hierarchy of the community. Among Protestant Crestwood Heighters, adherence to a specific church "is more a matter of habit than deep conviction, a socially useful practice than a source of spiritual solace." [24] To the students of Elmtown, "the church is a community facility like the school, the drug store, the city government and the bowling alley," [25] and "adolescents deeply involved with church groups are interested in their clubs for social rather than religious reasons." [26] In Middletown, "in certain prominent business-class churches, girls' Sunday school classes, led by socially-prominent women, have become social sifting devices for the tightly competitive girls' club life in high school." [27]

Hollingshead came across one Methodist minister in Elmtown who had tried to organize his students into "one happy family working for Christ and the Church" but had "failed utterly." [28] The young people's organizations, sponsored by the church, though integrated nominally around religion and religious objectives, "in essence promote primarily the clique interests of their members." [29] The girls in one high-status church club "make any girl of whom they do not approve feel so uncomfortable that she will attend neither young people's meetings nor Sunday School." [30] Similarly in Jonesville, W. Lloyd Warner and his group discovered that one minister, in the high-status Federated Church, "failed to realize that his troubles, which ultimately led to forcing his resignation, were the result of the great class spread in his church. He tried unsuccessfully to increase attendance and activity in various auxiliaries. He was blocked time after time by the class differences of the members." [31] Cliques in the men's and women's groups and Sunday School classes forced the lower-status members out. In Middletown, the Lynds discovered an identical situation: high-school cliques were based on which Sunday School the participants attended and, as one teenager told the investigators, "the poorest kids are separated off." [32]

One can scarcely blame the adolescents for aping the adult world of religion. It is ironic but undeniable that the Christian Church, in which all men are supposed to be equal in their humility before God, is as much obsessed with status as any major social institution. The Church's failure of leadership in the racial crisis is understandable when one observes the segregation within the churches themselves. I do not mean racial segregation here; that is obvious enough. I mean segregation by economic and social class. The churches in Jonesville, U.S.A., "the City of the Common Man," are, in the words of those who studied the city for several years, "clearly influenced by social class attitudes. The upper, middle and lower classes favour certain churches and avoid others." [33] So clearly defined is the class system that Warner in Jonesville and Hollingshead in Elmtown were able to make caste charts categorizing each denomination by its relative position on the ladder of status. Vance Packard dealt with the matter at length in *The Status Seekers,* categorizing the major Protestant sects in order of class importance. He began with the Episcopalians (favoured by corporation executives, Social Register members, *Who's Who* listees and society-page "names") and worked down through the Presbyterian, Congregationalists, Methodists, Lutherans, Baptist, Pentecostal, and Holiness sects, in that exact descending order.[34] Packard's evidence is impressive enough to justify his question: "Should one be worshipping in a setting that makes a mockery of one of the core values of Christianity: the brotherhood of man?" and Packard adds: "At present the brotherhood of man is in danger of becoming merely a nice intellectual concept." [35]

Liston Pope, a former Dean of the Yale Divinity School, came to similar conclusions before Packard. In 1948, he reported to the American Academy of Political and Social Science that "differentiation within Protestantism corresponds fairly closely to class divisions. Individual Protestant churches tend to be 'class churches,' with members drawn principally from one class group." [36] Even when membership cut across class lines, Dr. Pope discovered, the control of the church was in the hands of one class. Pointing out that Christianity began among the poor, Pope said that the Church today, having permeated the higher classes, has "relatively neglected the poor," and that "unless a drastic transformation comes about in the churches, they will probably continue for the most part to adapt to class divisions—and even intensify them—as they have done in the past."

This Balkanization of the Church is not entirely casual or subconscious, as Warner discovered when he and a research team studied another modern American community, which they called Yankee City. The two upper-class churches in that city had worked out a method of limiting the membership of lower classes in their congregations by the expedient gimmick of establishing branches in other parts of the city that served as lower-class missions. Thus were the unwashed effectively constrained from wandering into the stained-glass ghetto which the best people had built for themselves in the privileged section of the community.[37]

"The capitalistic aspect of Protestantism is such that those who are the most privileged have the best churches, the finest plants, the ablest leadership, while those who are most needful have the minimum of resources both of plant and staff." [38] So wrote Stanley North, Director of the Department of City Works, New York. But the evil is not confined to the urban communities of this continent. J. B. Phillips in his book about the mission of the Christian Church, *The Church Under the Cross,* quotes a villager in India: "We would become Christians but for the caste prejudices of the

Christians in this village, which would make it impossible for us to worship with them." Phillips points out that most Christians view the Indian caste system as thoroughly repugnant, yet when the British class system was at its most rigid, "very little voice was raised in the Church of England to point out the evils of snobbery, social pride and the idea that God himself had arranged that people should be born in distinct social strata." [39]

The Christian faith, in short, which in its beginnings was anything but respectable, is now the basis on which community respectability and prestige rests.* My own observation and opinion is that, in the matter of church unity, it is really class differences rather than basic doctrinal differences that frustrate an ecumenical solution to Christian fragmentation.

The unconscious class attitudes of church leaders is never better illustrated than in the matter of military service. I have always found it slightly ironic that Christian ministers who join the army to minister to the troops automatically become members of the officer caste. If Christ were a chaplain, would he eat in the officers' mess? It is hardly likely. Yet Waldo W. Burchard, in his postwar sociological study of American military chaplains, discovered that more than ninety per cent of the respondents in his sample reported that they did not feel out of place as officers.[40] Burchard added that "only two respondents appeared to fit the popular stereotype of the chaplain as the champion of the enlisted men." Why? Because "if the chaplain were to sympathize too openly with enlisted personnel . . . he might lose caste with his fellow officers." [41]

The evil of caste is that it freezes the opinions and outlooks of its members. Only by remaining outside the caste system, only by resisting the temptations of those who are status-conscious, can

---

* It is interesting, in this context, to examine the history of one of the most famous Methodist families in Canada, the Masseys. When the Massey farm-implement fortune was being accumulated, the Methodist church was traditionally the refuge of the small and aggressive businessman, while the Anglican church was the preserve of the privileged classes. It is perhaps germane to note that, as the Masseys rose in social prestige, several of them joined the higher-status church. These include the Rt. Hon. Vincent Massey, the former Governor General, now a "high" Anglican, and his well-known cousin, Denton, the former evangelistic leader of the Methodist-oriented York Bible Class, who has been ordained an Anglican priest.

the modern clergyman hope to keep his mind from becoming shackled by the opinions of the peer group. If he worships at the altar of status, the Christian leader must compartmentalize his mind in exactly the same way that the Japanese do.

Burchard discovered that the views of the chaplains he surveyed differed in no way from those of other officers on the deep question of the morality of modern warfare. More than half, in fact, denied that any conflict existed between military regulations and religious ideology; seventy-nine per cent believed that a man with a good religious training would make a better soldier; forty-five per cent went along with the view that killing an enemy soldier was a righteous act, and the remainder thought it justifiable; *none* felt that the individual soldier had any moral responsibility in the matter except to serve his country.[42] This outlook is very similar to the one that formed the core of Adolph Eichmann's defence during his trial in Israel.

Burchard reported, significantly, that compartmentalization of the mind was the escape technique used by most chaplains to reconcile disparities between military and religious teaching. Again we face the Orwellian horror of *doublethink*.

Some idea of the pressures that the need for social conformity can bring, when the Christian Church is faced with a major social issue, can be gleaned from an important study of the racial crisis in Little Rock. The study was conducted by two sociologists from Harvard's Laboratory of Social Affairs. The investigators came to these conclusions (among others) regarding the role of Christian ministers in this, the first school desegregation crisis:

> The more popular the denomination in the local area, the less likely are its ministers to defend positions not accepted by local public opinion.
>
> The minister is less likely to support desegregation during a crisis if no ministerial figures of high prestige in his denomination lead the way.
>
> The minister's support of desegregation is less if his church is engaged in a membership drive, building program or fund-raising campaign than if it is not so engaged.
>
> The more stable the membership of his church, the less likely is the minister to support desegregation during a crisis period.

Success (speaking numerically and financially) in the ministry is negatively related to the probability of strong advocacy of unpopular moral imperatives.[43]

The researchers came to the conclusion that many ministers were justifying their lack of social action in order "to preserve the church as a church . . . to maintain church unity and with it an institutional program." Certain institutional characteristics of the modern church made it important "to preserve a frictionless congregation," and this responsibility took "precedence over any desire to effectuate social reform." [44]

In short, the maintenance of the religious establishment has become an end in itself and not a means, something more important than Christian principle, Christian action, or even real Christian brotherhood.

3   RELIGION VERSUS CHRISTIANITY

THE WORSHIP OF CONFORMITY and respectability, which distinguishes the religious establishment, turns religion and Christianity into two separate entities. Religion, the cult of the establishment, with its denial of Christian radicalism, its alliance with the status quo and its awesome social power, is, indeed, often the antithesis of Christianity. Kierkegaard saw this clearly a century ago when he wrote with bitterness that the priests of the establishment were anxious that every Dane should call himself a Christian in order that the numerical strength of Christians might contribute to the power of the clerical order.

"Nothing," he wrote, "is more dangerous to true Christianity, nothing more contrary to its nature, than to get men to assume light-mindedly the name of Christian . . . as if it were something one is as a matter of course. And the priest is particularly interested in having it stop there . . . that men should not learn to know what Christianity truly is, for with that the whole machinery with the nine-thousand officials and state power to back them up would go up in the air. . . ." [45]

Were the great philosopher alive today in North America, his outrage would scarcely be contained. For truly, in issues of universal brotherhood, "religion" seems to deny the Christian message. Gordon W. Allport's classic study *The Nature of Prejudice* is one that demonstrates how the religious are far more racially and ethnically prejudiced than the non-religious. Church members, for one thing, are more prejudiced, Allport finds, than non-church members. [46] Among a sample of college students, those reporting that religion has been a marked or moderate influence in their lives show a far higher degree of prejudice than those who report that religion was either slight or non-existent in their upbringing. [47] But Allport is careful to point out that it is the "institutional type of attachment, external and political in nature," that turns out to be associated with prejudice; truly devout laymen, as opposed to the institutionalized kind, were found to have less prejudice. [48]

Allport puts it succinctly: "Belonging to a church because it is a safe, powerful, superior in-group is likely to be the mark of an authoritarian character and to be linked with prejudice. Belonging to a church because its basic creed of brotherhood expresses the ideals one sincerely believes in is associated with tolerance." [49]

Similar conclusions were arrived at by the team of scholars that undertook the massive study of latent fascist tendencies in individuals, which they published under the title of *The Authoritarian Personality*. "Belonging to or identifying oneself with a religious body in America today certainly does not mean that one thereby takes over the traditional Christian qualities of tolerance, brotherhood and equality," they wrote. "On the contrary, it appears that these values are more firmly held by people who do not affiliate with any religious group. It may be that religious affiliation or church attendance is of little importance one way or the other in determining social attitudes, that the great majority of Americans identify themselves with some religious denomination as a matter of course, *without thinking much about it*." [50] (Italics mine.)

These conclusions were arrived at after exhaustive studies of a large sample whose views both conscious and subconscious were measured through depth interviews and Thematic Apperception Tests. The investigators worked out two scales of measurement: an "A-S" scale to measure specific anti-Semitic tendencies among their subjects; and a broader "E" scale to measure ethnocentric tendencies involving authoritarian, fascist-oriented and generally prejudiced attitudes against all minority or "out" groups. High scores indicated a high degree of prejudice and ethnocentrism; low scores, tolerance.

The results were significant. Those who rejected organized religion had much lower scores on both scales, indicating less prejudice and more tolerance than those who accepted religion. Those who blindly accepted their parents' religion had much higher scores than those who were either in revolt against religion or who accepted religion independently of parental influence as a result of their own conclusions and decisions. The researchers reported that "the fact of acceptance or rejection of religion is not as important as the *way* in which it is accepted or rejected." [51] Those with a relatively personalized or internalized religion scored much lower than those who accepted religion as a matter of convention. There was a much greater degree of anti-Semitism among those who considered religion and the church important than among those who either felt it was unimportant or "emphasized the ethical aspects of religion or differentiated between the church and 'real' religion and, while rejecting the former, stressed the more personal and the more rational aspects of the latter." [52] Here the difference between the attitudes of the nominally religious and the committed Christians is easily observable.

The authors of *The Authoritarian Personality* draw a parallel with the radical Christian movement in Nazi Germany, which produced such men as Karl Barth, who courageously opposed the Nazi establishment. Such groups, who "take religion seriously," are likely to be opposed to all forms of ethnocentrism. On the other hand "to put it bluntly, the adherent of what Kierkegaard . . . called 'official Christianity' is likely to be ethnocentric although the religious organizations with which he is affiliated may be officially opposed to it, whereas the 'radical' Christian is prone to think and to act differently." [53]

Somewhat similar results have been obtained from studies of attitudes toward peace, war, disarmament, and world government. A study in 1962 of 437 residents of Northampton, Mississippi, showed that those most apt to see the possibility of war, those most apt to favour a fall-out shelter program, those most apt to believe that communism was an evil that must be stamped out, were also highest in "religiosity." [54] An even more recent study of Canadian attitudes, by the Canadian Peace Research Institute under the direction of Dr. Jerome Lauchlicht, a New York sociologist, suggests that the sense of responsibility toward one's fellow men is more pronounced among non-churchgoers.[55] "I kept looking for little tinges of basic Christianity among those who attended church regularly," Lauchlicht told me, when he was putting the results of his depth interviews through computers. "I found nothing." In his study, regular churchgoers were found more likely to favour nuclear weapons, less likely to worry about the spread of these weapons, more hostile to any talk of negotiation, peace discussions, or interaction between cold-war opponents, were less fearful of the results of the arms race, and were more "deterrent-minded" than the reluctant or non-churchgoer.

Yet regular churchgoing and public adherence to the institutionalized side of religion is a social requirement enforced by a religious establishment. Though Christ clearly intended the opposite, churchgoing appears to put more emphasis on formalized religious observance than it does on ethical relationships. Though the Sabbath and the Church were made for man and not man for the Sabbath, most ministers continue to affirm that you cannot be a good Christian unless you attend church regularly. When the Church gets involved, as it occasionally does, with the mass media, this is the essence of its advertising message. "Attend the church of your choice" is the slogan and not "Love one another." *

---

* It is significant that Stan Freberg's widely publicized religious-advertising jingles, used by the Anglican and the United Church on Canadian radio stations in 1964, made no mention of any Christian virtues but simply emphasized the usefulness of the church to the individual: "Doesn't it get a little lonely sometimes out on a limb without Him? . . . Why try to go it alone? The blessings you lose may be your own. . . . It's a great life but it could

The religious establishment exerts great power in the community and brings great pressure to bear upon those who resist it. In Elmtown, "to be labelled a church member is very important, for it tells people where one belongs. . . . One can refer to himself as being of any Christian faith without inciting outright opposition. . . . However, if he blandly says that he is an atheist, barriers will be erected around him . . . for atheist and communist are two labels an Elmtowner must avoid if he desires to be accepted as a respectable member of society." [56] Teachers in Elmtown schools are watched carefully by church leaders who question young people about statements made in class relative to the Bible and religion. Pressure is often brought on the Board of Education against teachers making "irreligious" statements. "If a church cannot achieve its ends through the Board, sometimes its representatives wait upon an offender personally and lay down its demands." [57]

It sometimes seems as if the atheist has fewer rights today in the United States than the Negro; few aspiring job-seekers would dare identify themselves as atheists on application forms. Indeed, an attempt was made in 1964 to exclude atheists from that section of the American civil-rights bill that guarantees equal-employment opportunities. Such an amendment to Title VII of the bill, which would have made second-class citizens of Benjamin Franklin, Thomas Jefferson, Tom Paine, Thomas Edison, and Albert Einstein, was indeed accepted by the House of Representatives by a vote of 173-98, though it was not included in the final version of the bill passed by the Senate. It is significant that a companion amendment, again accepted by the House, also disbarred Communists from equal job opportunities. Increasingly atheists are being lumped together with "Godless Communists," so that communism and atheism are often seen as the same thing. Any man who overtly disaffiliates himself from official religion be-

---

be greater. Where'd you get the idea you could make it by yourself?" In all these slogans there is the implicit suggestion that the church can be used as a crutch for a "greater life," to combat loneliness, to gain "blessings." The prospective church-attender is offered a series of bribes but is asked to give nothing in return.

comes politically suspect, while those who pay lip service to any denomination perform, in effect, an act of allegiance. Thus does the religious establishment confuse religion with patriotism.

In T. W. Adorno's words, religion, having been deprived of the intrinsic claim to truth, "has gradually been transformed into 'social cement.'"

> The more this cement is needed for the maintenance of the *status quo* and the more dubious its inherent truth becomes, the more obstinately is its authority upheld and the more its hostile, destructive and negative features come to the fore. The transformation of religion into an agency of social conformity makes it fall in line with most other conformist tendencies. Adherence to Christianity under such conditions easily lends itself to abuse; to subservience, overadjustment, and ingroup loyalty as an ideology that covers up hatred against the disbeliever, the dissenter, the Jew.[58]

The same point was made in a different way by a United Church minister in an Ontario community who recently wrote me:

> I know a teacher who is in a small town in which he doesn't dare not go to church because it is socially unacceptable to be a public agnostic. I'm certain he has let the presiding clergyman know of his position, but preachers are loath to lose pew-fodder or to do anything to harm the position of phoney prestige which the Church occupies as a social institution. Similarly, there are people in our town who are agnostics or atheists, who have to send their children to Sunday School because the pressure brought to bear, for example, on children in kindergarten by those who show very little influence of Christian charity when they encounter a weirdy who doesn't go to Sunday School and doesn't know the stupid songs and stories we have left over from the Old-Time Religion.

In many parts of the country (it was true of both Great Britain and the Province of Ontario until 1964), a childless couple cannot adopt a child without producing proof of some religious affiliation. Again, it is often religious agencies that have helped screen candidates for admission into the country and become responsible for them afterwards.* The effect is not to aid the spread of Christianity but merely to increase the hypocrisy of thousands who are forced to pretend to a religious faith in order to gain a practical end.

The establishment thus perpetuates itself at the cost of the faith, and this is true in that other area of power and pressure, religious education in the schools. To this concept the churches cling so tenaciously that one might think their very fate hung upon its continuation. Yet Alasdair MacIntyre's remarks on the situation in Great Britain (not very different from the situation in several Canadian provinces) seem to me to point out the basic flaws of religious instruction in public schools.

It is just not true that children in this country are indoctrinated in Christianity as a result of the 1944 Education Act. What they *are* indoctrinated in is confusion. This confusion is rooted in the fact that on one hand religious instruction is compulsory and yet on the other it is clear that the schools do not take it seriously in the way they do basic literature or subjects such as history or chemistry.

The comprehensive survey of students' confused attitudes to Christianity to be found in Harold Loukes's *Teen Age Religion*[59] bears this out. The teaching of religion in secular schools clearly does not work, as a majority of delegates to the British Columbia Teachers' Federation Convention in 1964 made clear; but anyone who opposes it does so at his peril. He will come under heavy attack from the religious establishment; he will be reviled as "Godless"; his morality, his loyalty, his sincerity and even his politics will be questioned. I speak from personal experience.

* The power of the religious establishment in Canada and the necessity of paying lip service to conventional beliefs came to light in September 1964, when it was revealed that a Dutch couple, Mr. and Mrs. Ernest Bergsma of Caledonia, had been refused Canadian citizenship after ten years' residence. A study of the exchange in Hansard between the justice minister, Guy Favreau, and members of both opposition parties, makes it clear that the paramount reason for the Bergsmas' rejection was their professed atheism.

The insistence upon, and the espousal of, so-called "religious" instruction in the schools* underlines the long-term alliance between the religious establishment and the political establishment. It is time for the Church to question whether this alliance is a good thing for Christianity.

"With some individual exceptions," Bertrand Russell writes me, "the Anglican Church has upheld every Government view including those concerning war and killing. The Church is a force for established opinion and resistance to conscientious protest." This is a savage indictment but a true one. It applies to other church establishments in other lands at other periods in history: to the Church which was an ally of a brutal feudal system; to the Lutheran Church in Germany during the rise of Hitler; to the Catholic Church which was the partner of fascism in Italy and Spain; to the major Protestant Churches in the United States which transferred their allegiance to a national concept so that religion becomes part of an "okay" world, as represented by a dozen clean-cut Billy Graham figures who enlist God as an ally of the CIA in the battle against communism, and enrol thousands of statistical Christians to make their "decision" for Christ—a form of Instant Religion which, apparently in a flash, transforms them from nominal sinners into socially respectable citizens.

"Religion," of course, has always been the basis in any society of moral order, of law, of responsibility. What is moral and what is respectable, however, differ from society to society and from age to age. Though religion may be able to support a system of social morals at any given period, it is questionable whether Christianity can. For Christianity is supposed to be a religion with a difference. It is a universal religion—universal in time and universal in space. That being so, how can it survive if it tries to be

---

* I say "so-called" because it is, in effect, not religious instruction at all but instruction in the broad principles of the majority Protestant sects only. Vast numbers of children who attend the public schools—Jewish, Roman Catholic, Unitarian, Adventist, Mennonite, Quaker, Christian Scientist—to name a few—are given "instruction" that may not be compatible with their beliefs and which has, on occasion, proven embarrassing to some. They must accept it or else accept the often equally embarrassing alternative of "opting out."

the basis of a fleeting social respectability? If Christianity becomes merely a passport to status and prestige in various societies, then it will surely wither away.

4 THE CASTING OUT OF THE OUTCASTS

IN THE BEGINNING, Christianity was anything but a respectable creed. Its founder moved among the outcasts of society—among the prostitutes, racial minorities, political traitors, misfits, vagrants, and thieves; among "the hungry, the naked, the homeless, and the prisoner." He himself was considered a religious heretic and a traitor to his nation, an enemy of the status quo, a man who broke the Sabbath, a dangerous radical, a disturber and a malcontent who fought the establishment and whose constant companions were the sort of people who are to be found today in the skid-row areas of the big cities. When he stood trial, there was an element of truth in the charge under which he was indicted: "He stirreth up the people."

One could scarcely call him success-motivated. Not only by present standards but also by those of his own time, he was a total failure. He went to his degrading death broken and beaten, cast out by respectable society, spat upon and cursed by the righteous, and reviled by all save the handful of malcontents who, like himself, were beyond society's pale. It appeared, when he died, that he had accomplished nothing. Indeed, it would have been difficult to prepare a suitable caption to publish beneath his photograph in any diocesan monthly, had such a publication existed in his time.

It has been said, with truth (and by a Christian minister), that none of the twelve apostles would feel at home today in a modern church. Nor is it likely that a modern church would welcome the kind of people with whom its founder associated.

August Hollingshead, who divided Elmtown's prestige-structure into five distinct castes—Class V was "looked upon as the scum of the city by the higher Classes" [60]—reported that nine out of ten Class V families had no active connection with the Church and ninety-eight per cent of all Class V fathers either were not known to the ministers or did not attend church if they were known.[61] Active hostility to the Church was encountered frequently: "One woman epitomized the situation when she said bitterly, 'The "Everyone Welcome" signs in front of the churches should add "except people like us"—we're not wanted.' She was right—they are not wanted by the congregations, and several of the ministers in the high-prestige churches do not encourage their attendance." [62] To a large segment of the young people of the lower classes, "the church, the preacher, and the outwardly pious members of the church boards represent the acme of hypocrisy." [63] For the church elders, the pew-warmers, and the plate-passers do not rub shoulders with the kind of man whom Christ welcomed as a brother, and the religious establishment no longer identifies itself with the man in the gutter, with the convict, the thief, the prostitute, the political radical, or the real social outcasts of our time.*

Who are these outcasts? Who are the modern lepers from whom society cringes, crying out "Unclean! Unclean!" Is it possible that the Church no longer recognizes them? Recently a sample of 248 Anglican ministers across Canada was asked the following question as part of a larger survey of attitudes: "In his day, Christ moved with the outcasts of society—the lepers, prostitutes, tax collectors, etc. What group or groups would you say constituted the outcasts of society today?"

Varieties of answers were given, many of which suggested that the clergymen in question had no real understanding of the mean-

---

* There are, as always, some refreshing exceptions to this general attitude that ought to be commended. A dozen laymen from the Church of the Holy Trinity, Toronto, an Anglican congregation largely composed of middle-class suburban families who travel downtown for Sunday service, have recently established a mission in the tenderloin district of Toronto. The church is responsible for this, but until very recently had done little about it. The laymen and their priest, the Reverend James Fisk, now go to the mission twice each week to mingle with the men who are unemployed and often alcoholic. Wisely, they do not talk about religion unless asked. Appropriately, the mission is situated in an old beverage room.

ing of the word "outcast" in its Christian context. (Among the "outcasts" mentioned as groups were "those happy on welfare," "newly rich," "unacademic teenagers," "common-law wives," "early school dropouts," "women who work and don't need to," "low-income families with low standards of morals" and even "tax collectors.") Others gave the standard answers: eighty-one ministers mentioned alcoholics; eighty-one mentioned racial minorities; sixty-four listed legal offenders of various kinds; forty-seven referred, in several ways, to the poor and the indigent; forty-six mentioned the sick, especially the mentally ill; thirty-five referred to prostitutes. These are, in general, the traditional outcasts of Biblical times—the Samaritans and sinners, the sick, the naked, and the homeless. But are they the true outcasts of our era? In an era of Mental Health and Brotherhood weeks, Alcoholics Anonymous conventions, Community Chest and United Appeal drives, are these people universally shunned in the way the lepers of old were shunned?

I find it significant that only twenty-six ministers specifically mentioned the homosexual, and that of 248 ministers questioned only four had made any mention of the homosexual in a sermon during the previous six months. Yet a very good case can be made out that the homosexual is the modern equivalent of the leper. His very job, economic and social status, community position, and public acceptance depend on the successful concealment of an awful secret. And when his disease is discovered, he is relegated to the modern leper colony—the half-world of his fellows which, with great irony and great sadness, is called "gay."

That homosexuals themselves feel ignored and rejected by the Church is beyond doubt. Here is the president of Canada's largest homosexual colony, a Yonge Street club in Toronto, talking:

You just don't get anywhere with the Church. We asked four or five ministers to come down and speak to us, but they refused. They were afraid of causing controversy. They were afraid of adverse reactions from their congregations. Some said they couldn't do anything because the Church had laid down definite lines and they would be reprimanded—so what was the use? Many of our members have been active in the Church in their younger days, but when the Church rejects them they reject the Church; and our experience is that Protestants reject homosexuals. Those who are active in the Church don't admit that they are homosexual. The rest stay away from the Church. They know what's going to happen if they try to go, so they just don't bother. What would be the point?

It is now becoming apparent that the homosexual may be remarkably similar to the leper of Biblical times—a sick man unable to control the ravages of a disease that is itself misunderstood. "They are all sick people," says Dr. Stephen Neiger, a senior psychologist of the Toronto Psychiatric Hospital. "Homosexuals must be regarded as we regard the alcoholic and the drug addict." But society does not so regard them; nor does the Church. They are sinners and they are beyond the pale. It is true that some churches, including the Anglican Church, have one or two priests who do minister to groups that include homosexuals. It is also true that the Granite Club of Toronto is said to have one or two Jewish members. This does not absolve the Granite Club from the valid charge of discrimination, and it does not absolve the Church from the valid charge that it has not only neglected these modern outcasts but has also taken part in their persecution.

"The persecution of homosexuals," says Peter Berger, "is so vicious for very much the same reason that racial persecution is. While a persecutor in the latter case uses his victim in bad faith to bolster his spurious self-identification as a member of a superior race, the persecutor in the former case forces upon himself and his victim the confirmation of his own usually shaky self-identification as a 'normal' male. One beats the Negro to feel white. One spits upon the homosexual to feel virile." [64]

It is not without significance that some of the Christian ministers who refused to speak to the homosexual club said that they did so because they feared similar tendencies in themselves. They would not touch the lepers for fear of contracting the disease.

5 THE COMFORTABLE PEW

IT HAS ALL but been forgotten that Christianity began as a revo-
lutionary religion whose followers embraced an entirely different
set of values from those held by other members of society. Those
original values are still in conflict with the values of contemporary society; yet religion today has become as conservative a
force as the force the original Christians were in conflict with.

Why is it that the Church today is afraid to speak loudly and
with a radical voice? Perhaps it is because the Church, like so
many of its members, is afraid to look ridiculous. It ought to be
making front-page headlines regularly by advocating what is absolutely counter to the general thrust of society; but it does not
do so. How many Christian ministers today go to jail for their
beliefs? How many make the kind of physical protest that puts
them outside the bounds of the social order? Most, in Gordon
Allport's words, become "defenders of a culture." In defending
the absolutes of their faith, they tend to defend their in-group as
a whole, "finding in the absolutes of their faith justification for
the secular practices of their in-group." [65] The institution of
religion, which once generated its own values, now merely gives
its blessing to the majority-held values of the community around
it.

It is easier, of course, to see this conservatism, this identification with the in-group, this terror of being "way out," in operation
in a social environment other than one's own. A young Canadian
girl named Mary Suzuki was recently appalled by an experience
she had with ministers of various faiths during a Peace March
from Montreal to Cuba. The marchers, all members of the Committee for Non-Violent Action, encountered trouble in Albany,
Georgia, because they were an integrated group, some white and
some Negro. The authorities refused to give them a permit to

walk through the business district, and as a result demonstrations, jail sentences, and hunger strikes followed. Miss Suzuki and her friends appealed to the local ministers for help.

"We simply said to the ministers what they had been saying to their congregations about brotherly love," Miss Suzuki told me. "When they heard that, they ran. They didn't even want to talk to us. I remember one man we tried to see who insisted he was all booked up with appointments. We persisted, and finally he saw us reluctantly. We ended up talking for four hours. He was sympathetic, too. But he refused to take any action."

Miss Suzuki, who calls herself an atheist, was here acting in the traditional Christian manner; she and her friends were, in fact, walking sermons. It was they, and not the religious establishment, who were in a Christian conflict with society.

It is easy, of course, for a Canadian to attack Christian ministers in the deep South for not acting in the cause of universal Christian brotherhood. It is more difficult to contemplate direct action of a similar kind against the various sins of one's own community. What would be the general attitude, for instance, to a man who drove the modern usurers from their temples on Bay or King or Yonge Streets in Toronto? Suppose a man of the cloth stormed into the posh offices of one of the several loan companies, whose rates on second mortgages or automobiles have gone higher than thirty per cent, smashed their furniture and drove them from the premises with a whip? Suppose a leading clergyman strode into one of the several dozen used-car lots in this nation that make a practice of cheating their customers and horsewhipped the owner? Suppose a bishop physically attacked a bailiff for evicting a poor family? How would society treat such men? How would their congregations view them? What would the law do? And how many parishioners would visit their pastor if they had to meet him in the local jail or the local mental home?

When the Lynds revisited Middletown, they came to the conclusion that the role of religion was "not to raise troublesome questions and to force attention to disparities between values and current practice." [66] Religion in Middletown had become "an emotionally stabilizing agent." One of its leading ministers, speaking to the Kiwanis Club, frankly declared, "In the old days people went to preachers for consolation, information, and inspiration. They still come to us for consolation, but go to newspapers for information and inspiration." [67]

Institutional Christianity, in short, has become a comfortable creed, a useful tool for Peace of Mind and Positive Thinking, a kind of sugar-coated pill that soothes those who fear to face the traditional Christian concerns of evil, suffering, and death—concerns, be it said, that have been miraculously minimized and glossed over by the religious establishment.

Vance Packard, in a skeptical assessment, has written that "while the lower-class religions offer consolation for failure, many (but not all) upper-class churches tend to generate the pleasant feeling that everything within the social system is pretty fine as it is." [68] Religion, in today's society, provides a cotton-wool haven for those who cannot face the kind of truths that the apostles had to face. It is epitomized in those cheerful painting of a non-suffering Saviour, that hang in so many homes and stare out of so many Sunday School tracts—recently described by Dan Wakefield in *The Nation* in a cutting review of the new Methodist magazine *Together*.[69]

Wakefield pointed out that through the ages our image of Christ has grown progressively healthier and happier. There was the deeply troubled and meditative second-century portrait, the forehead scarred, the lips turned downward. There was the dark, stern face of the eleventh-century Messiah. Then there was the weeping Christ, blood-spattered, found in sixteenth-century paintings. All these have been supplanted by the early twentieth-century representation, which shows a glow emerging from the unlined forehead, and by the current, curly-haired, pink-cheeked, smiling Saviour, "his brow shorn of scars and sorrows." This Christ seems to fit in with the Methodist concept of the ideal boy friend, as described in *Together* ("Can he earn a reasonably good living? Does he have a stable personality?"), or the first All-American Methodist football team ("conforms to [the] requisites of success") or one of the magazine's clerical authors ("looks like a successful lawyer and talks like the man next door")—in short, a Christ who, in Wakefield's words, has "a face indistinguishable from the rest of the lonely crowd."

The radicals within the Church from Kierkegaard to Bonhoeffer have rejected this comfortable version of Christ, as they have rejected the idea that the Christian religion can be a comfortable one, in the modern definition of that abused word. And this surely suggests the basic difference between the kind of religion the establishment practises and true Christianity, which came into being as a difficult, dangerous, radical, uncomfortable, shattering, but also vastly stimulating and exciting way of life.

The establishment's religion is one that calls upon the deity as a servant in peace and war. It can be discovered in the blasphemy of Norman Vincent Peale's "cult of reassurance," in which Christianity becomes a mere vehicle on the road to worldly success, and "faith" a kind of super-aspirin that can be painlessly swallowed to provide fast, fast, fast relief from the burning issues of our time. It is the kind of religion that allows an official of a Canadian hockey team, in an emotion-choked voice, to credit his win over the Russians to God, prayer, and constant Bible reading or permits Field Marshal Montgomery to call on the Almighty as one of the chief architects of Allied victory.

But the Christian God is surely something more than a useful tool for winning wars and hockey games or gaining an advantage in the business world. Man, we were once told, was made to serve God and not God man; which is perhaps another way of saying that man ought to have some humility about him. Nor is God merely a facile witchdoctor, useful for getting rid of headaches and heartaches. It is true that those who are weary and heavy laden are invited to seek him out for comfort. It is also true that the word "comfort" has changed with the growth of the affluent society. In its original meaning—in the Biblical sense—"comfort" implied fortitude. It in no sense connoted the cosy "peace of mind" that the modern Church is clearly supposed to dispense like so much soothing syrup; it implied a sterner kind of strengthening aid, which allowed the supplicant not to forget his sorrows and sufferings, but to come to terms with them, to face up to them, and to carry on.

It is precisely this quality of being able to come to grips with despair, rather than hiding from it like a child beneath bedsheets, that has always separated the men from the boys in a harsh, unfriendly world. But the religious establishment persists in treating men like boys, as it once treated natives like children. It forgets that, in two thousand years of Christianity, the human race has grown, changed and achieved adulthood; that it has learned something about the external world: about the nature of the heavens above and the earth beneath and the mysteries of creation; that it has also learned something about the internal world: the nature of the mind and perhaps even of the soul, and the nature of birth and of heredity and of life itself. The Church has always embraced this new knowledge reluctantly and tardily, and it is a comment on the attitudes of the religious establishment that Copernicus, Darwin, Freud, and all their disciples have each been in conflict with it.

Now in the second half of the most mercurial century in the Christian epoch, at the beginning of the New Age, the Church still resists the change in men's minds. It is not merely that the Church's techniques and its language belong to a forgotten era making its message murky; it is also that the Church stands in danger of forgetting exactly what that message is.

THREE

THE FAILURE OF COMMUNICATION

I
PRETENSIONS TO ABSOLUTE RIGHTNESS

2
THE SPECIAL LANGUAGE OF PRIESTHOOD

3
THE LUKEWARM PULPIT

4
THE REJECTION OF TWENTIETH-CENTURY MEDIA

5
FAITH WITHOUT DOGMA

Why are you not saying what you ought to say and saying it with power and eloquence? Why don't you force us to pay attention to you and listen to you? We should like to see you less timid, more consistent, bolder. We often have the impression you are afraid—of what, really? And you spread so little light and joy around you. When you make yourselves heard it is usually with cares, complaints, lamentations and accusations. . . .

Karl Barth in a BBC Address[1]

1 PRETENSIONS TO ABSOLUTE RIGHTNESS

"IT IS NOT an accident," writes Peter Berger in *The Precarious Vision,* "that the most rapidly growing religious bodies in America today are those with the most grandiose pretensions to absolute rightness." [2] When Christianity becomes part of the religious and social establishment, when it weaves itself into the national creed, it becomes an inflexible religion, suffering truly from a kind of "rightness" that renders it disdainful of new conditions, mores, habits, or attitudes. It looks back upon the past rather than forward into the future, until it becomes itself fossilized, using symbols and language no longer appropriate to its place and time.

We are now able to see fairly clearly that, in the past, certain Christian missionaries suffered from these "grandiose pretensions to absolute rightness"—from a form of snobbishness or smugness that, it seems to me, has for some time been part of the fabric of the religious establishment.

Imperialism, it has been said, begins with the missionary. If the missionary is unconscious of the fact that he is an advance scout for the political invader (as he certainly has been), this does not meliorate his error. The confusion between Western civilization and Christian civilization, between "Our Way of Life," so-called, and the Christian way of life, which has been so much a part of the present Cold War, really began some centuries ago in the age of exploration. For many generations, Christian missionaries operated in the absolute and disastrous conviction that what was good for British schoolboys or Boston matrons was also good for Chinese coolies, Hawaiian princesses, Indian rice farmers, and African tribesmen. Many Church people now recognize that this was true of another age and another place. But they fail to see that the same kind of inflexibility, the same refusal to adapt to native conditions, operates in the latter half of the twentieth century in Western society.

One of the most horrible photographs I have ever seen hangs in the little Polynesian museum in Papeete. It is a nineteenth-century official portrait of the Tahitian Royal Family. One stands there in the steaming tropical heat, dressed in nothing more than shorts and sandals, and looks with awe and compassion upon these sweltering natives decked out in black wool suits and vests, heavy shoes, stiff collars, thick ties, and hats—the prescribed Christian attire of the day—and one mourns for a creed so badly twisted that it could actually forbid, in the name of "morality," the wearing of the sensible native dress which, slightly altered, has become the uniform of every Western tourist. As Willis Church Lamott explains in his *Revolution in Missions,* the missionaries who set out to Christianize the Polynesians believed that Western civilization was a preparation for the gospel, and "that the noble truths of Christianity could not be apprehended until the way had been prepared by the softening effects of civilization." [3]

In East Africa, similar strictures were forced upon the natives by missionaries who failed to see either the significance or the value of local folkways. The Africans, for instance, were forbidden to express themselves in their own culture by playing their drums or other "pagan" instruments. The situation has changed in Africa, but in Canada the Church continues to show a marked reluctance to allow anything but organ music of another century and another culture within its walls. "Pagan" instruments, from the jazz clarinet and drums to the folk-singer's guitar, are frowned upon.

It may well be that the entire subcontinent of China was lost to Christendom because of this inflexibility. The first missionaries to that country in the sixteenth century attempted a bold experiment. They tried to preach only what they conceived to be the essence of the Christian religion—its universal truths—and to allow all external manners, fashions, mores, and customs to remain Chinese. Professor James Leyborn in *The Christian Century* has called this "a supreme example of clarity of vision and of Christian humility." [4] But the experiment was cut short on orders from the Vatican. The missionaries were told, in effect, that they must be agents of Western civilization, and as a result they were

soon expelled from China. Missionary work was not resumed for
almost three centuries, by which time the humiliation of China
and the concomitant disillusion with organized Christianity was
complete.

It has been salutary to note, of late, that some of the leaders of
the Church recognize this kind of problem. This was evident at
the Anglican Congress in Toronto, where the Bishop of Karachi
spoke out against "the image of the civilized missionary of superior faith coming to the heathen in darkness." [5] The ancient
drums have been returned to the African natives, and the attire in
Polynesia borrows as much from the South Pacific as it does from
Boston. "At long last," says Alec Graham, the Chaplain of
Worcestershire College, Oxford, "Christians are learning a little
humility." [6]

Yet in one sense the lesson has *not* been learned. The present
attack on all new forms of music and liturgy in the churches
sounds remarkably like the attack on native drums and flutes.
And one wonders whether there may not be a parallel between
the attitudes expressed by the missionaries to Tahitian clothing
and the glibly expressed antagonism of contemporary clergymen
who rushed, in the summer of 1964, to be quoted on the subject
of topless bathing suits—just as they rushed to be quoted, in
earlier decades but in almost identical terms, on the subject of
bikinis, two-piece suits, short skirts, women's slacks, peek-a-boo
shirt-waists, ankle-length dresses, and all the other style changes
that have slowly but inexorably unshackled the human body from
the imprisoning chain-mail of religious prudery.

The missionaries who leave the West to minister to other cul-
tures may have cast off the snobbishness and inflexibility of the
past; but how about the missionaries who have stayed behind?
One cannot escape the feeling that they tend to treat the members
of their congregations as small children, and one cannot help
agreeing with Bonhoeffer, who referred to "the attack by the
Christian apologetic on the adulthood of the world" [7]—an attack
which he called pointless, ignoble, and un-Christian.

This built-in snobbishness can be seen in some of the criticisms
of Bishop John Robinson's best-selling book *Honest to God*. The
Bishop has been chided within the Church, not because he said

anything that was theologically new, but because he said it in a paperback edition that anyone can purchase and read. The Rector of Birmingham called the book "a dangerous tract," apparently because "anyone . . . can easily buy it and read it and they probably will in great numbers." The Rector then goes on to say: "This is a pity because really the book is not intended for everyone. All parsons should read it and all well-educated laymen who are interested in Christianity. Other people may well be more hindered than helped by the tentative, exploratory, question-raising nature of the book." [8] As Bishop Robinson himself put it, rather wryly: " 'Not in front of the people' seems to be the unwritten rule of decent debate." [9]

This idea, held by the religious establishment, that certain truths and certain mysteries are too difficult to be understood by the masses, is not a new one; most aboriginal creeds hew to it. But it is surely the height of arrogance in an age of universal education and electronic mass media. If high-school students can be instructed in the elementals of Einsteinian mathematics, surely the average man is quite able to cope with the ancient mysteries of the faith and relate them to his own time. It has become a cliché of our age, which laymen, clergy, and free thinkers alike solemnly announce, that the Church is no longer able to communicate with the people. If this is true, and all the signs suggest that it is, it is because the Church no longer understands either the people or the modern science of communication. If its message is not outdated, its methods certainly are.

2 THE SPECIAL LANGUAGE OF PRIESTHOOD

MANY PEOPLE who no longer attend church, but who continue to call themselves Christian, give as a reason the fact that the service "does nothing for them." The liturgy is "dull and old-fashioned," the phraseology unfamiliar, the words archaic, the sermons cliché-ridden and irrelevant to the times, the organ music "square," the congregation spiritless. These, especially, are the comments of young people, as any random poll of youth—or a glance at the disproportionate number of elderly people in any of the major churches of a Sunday—will swiftly confirm.

Yet there was a time when the Church got its message across with colloquial music and language and with contemporary symbolism. Some of the hymns sung today were once the folk music of the people, just as the organ was *the* popular instrument. Such personal pronouns as "thee" and "thou" were part of everyday speech, as were verbs like "vouchsafe," "spake," and "beseech." The idiom has long since changed; the Church has not changed with it.

It is true that in recent times one or two churches have occasionally tried to incorporate jazz in their services. They have usually done it gingerly, not very well, and invariably to cries of protest. Yet why should not the Church once again use contemporary music to get its message across? What is wrong with a man with a guitar singing some new Christian folk songs relevant to the New Age? Is there anything really sinful about the presence of tenor sax, flute, clarinet, or drums in a church? Some would perhaps answer that all modern music is "bad" music or, at least, that much of it is coarse, transitory, or less than first rate. But the same adjectives apply to a good many of the more banal hymns, which congregations have been chanting lustily for more than a century.

Why do so many Christian services have to be so funereal? There was a time before the invention of the microphone, when many churches were more cavernous than they are today, when the man in the pulpit had to use a technique of voice-casting which, to modern ears, seems sepulchral. This is no longer necessary, yet many clergymen are still intoning their sermons and prayers in the singsong voice that has been the subject of so much recent stage parody.

Why must so much of the music be so dreary? Why is it not possible to use catchier, gayer tunes for at least some of the hymns? Why can't eternal truths be tied to a modern beat? Why is there an unwritten rule against jokes in the pulpit? Why cannot congregations join in with laughter and even applause? Is it really wrong for them to be involved in this way during a sermon? And why must clerics always be dressed in black during the course of their daily life? Oddly, the Saviour is never depicted in black. What Biblical or theological precept, then, rules that one's spiritual advisors must be dressed to resemble undertakers? If choir boys can sometimes wear scarlet, even occasionally in the United Church, why cannot a clergyman wear a crimson sports jacket?

The answer seems to be that the Protestant Church still clings to its sombre Puritan past. It still subconsciously believes that everything gay, lively, colourful, or enjoyable is somehow sinful. Fast, sprightly music is sinful; rhythm is especially sinful, since it connotes dancing; bright colours are sinful; jokes are sinful because they are frivolous, and all frivolity is, of course, sinful; adornment of all kinds is sinful. (Sex, it goes without saying, in all its manifestations is sinful, possibly because it is enjoyable.) Perhaps the Church no longer believes in these specifics, but the impression the Church gives to the world is that it does. Out of the dark recesses of its joyless past, these engrained notions emerge like small, elusive demons to haunt it. They have yet to be exorcised.

Has the Church forgotten that Christianity, in its original vision, is in no sense a doleful religion? With its inherent promise it resembles a marriage far more than a funeral. Why, then, does the Church make a virtue of black?

The answer may be that the Church's outer shell of liturgy, ritual, and myth has become fossilized. In the matter of language, for instance, the Church has become a prisoner of its own clichés. Words like "immanent," "justification," "sanctification," "atonement," "witness," "substitutionary sacrifice" and many, many others are as obscure to non-churchgoers as the jargon of Madison Avenue is incomprehensible to the clergy. It is no use saying that people *should* know what these words means; the truth is that they *don't* know. When the language is unintelligible, is it any wonder that the Church's attempts to reach the ear of modern man have so often failed?

In Paul Tillich's phrase, "Such words must be reborn." And if rebirth is impossible, then they must be thrown away, "even if they are protected by a long tradition." [10] But, as Tillich also says, it might be useful for the clergy themselves to ask each other what such words really mean in terms of modern life, whether they communicate something "infinitely important." One suspects that many of the in-group, who use old and worn-out phrases, are talking almost by rote, without having hacked through the thicket of cliché to get at the truth beneath. They really do not know what they are saying.

Again, one senses a kind of snobbishness in this. The special language of priesthood is, of course, an appurtenance of primitive religions. Witchdoctors, medicine men, and high priests make their authority felt through the mysteries of their language. There was a time in Christendom when, as John Lawrence, the editor of the Christian quarterly, *Frontier*, has written, "The higher reaches of religion were considered a special preserve of the clergy, sometimes almost a professional secret." [11] Indeed, it was considered a naughty thing for the masses to be able to read the Bible—it had to be interpreted for them. But it is surely an offence against the adulthood of the world for the modern Church to maintain a priestly jargon. By clinging to archaic words and an outmoded terminology, the Church has shown that it is not yet ready to join the New Age.

This general fossilization of language applies to the liturgy as a whole, and the evidence suggests that most of the clergy know about it. Out of a large sample of Anglican priests from across Canada who were questioned in the summer of 1964, 72.5 per cent felt that some change was needed in the liturgy. Of this group, a little more than half—fifty-five per cent—felt the changes required were only minor. But thirty-one per cent felt major changes were needed, and the remainder felt the changes should be drastic ones. Some of the comments were revealing: "The lessons should be written in language people understand. . . . Constant repetition tends to make any liturgy meaningless. . . . Our use of the liturgy is and ought to be a changing process. . . . The new prayer book is too conservative in language. . . . We spend half our bloody time explaining the prayer book instead of the gospel! Change to modern English!"

A report by one of the observers for the mass-observation study of the English industrial city Worktown, which I mentioned earlier, gives some idea of an outsider's view of one Anglican service. Noting that the hymnary contained verses first published in 1861, and that the prayer-book prayers dated back to 1928, this observer wrote:

I have never been to an Anglican service before and the division of time during the service struck me most. I felt that I was in a school where hymns were sung as a sort of exercise. I felt that at least three-quarters of the time was taken by singing hymns; there were five hymns altogether during the service and these had up to six verses. The songs are mostly sung by the choir to the congregation. I could not understand much of what was said by the priest or what was going on. There was no time for concentration on prayer or any other religious activity because all the hymns are sung standing up and if one was not standing up one was kneeling down or listening to the reading of the priest.

It was the fixed nature of the ritual that bothered this observer, especially the lack of any real spontaneity or any audience participation:

There was no action at all at the altar, which was completely empty and felt practically non-existent until at the very end the priest went up to the altar and prayed for a minute or two; he was praying in a very simple way for the Queen and Parliament and the sick and all the people to do with hospitals and so on. This form of prayer was the only *live* thing during the service. All the singing and announcements and reading was stereotyped and impressed me as doomed to failure, because there was no real connection between all that happened on the part of the choir boys and the priest and the people inside the church. It is more or less a routine taking place, which had lost the heart of the matter.[12]

In the winter of 1963-64, I decided to have another independent observer make a similar study of Anglican church services in the city of Toronto. I chose an intelligent woman in her early forties,

United Church by upbringing, mother of two children. I suggested that she attend either Matins or Evensong at upwards of a dozen churches in the various parts of the city, visiting those in the working-class districts, as well as in the upper-class residential areas and suburbs, choosing both "high" and "low" services. At the end of several months of weekly attendance, I asked this woman, who had never been to an Anglican service before this time, to sum up her views. Here is what she wrote:

"Most of all I failed to find an air of enthusiasm and vigour in the churches I attended. There is a dead-wood feeling about the whole service; an automatic and indifferent response on the part of the congregation, and an almost apologetic attitude in the delivery of the milk-and-water sermons on the part of the minister. The old-time preacher, long-winded and narrow-minded by today's standards, stood up and was counted no matter how unpopular his beliefs might be. In the last several months not one sermon has even touched on any of today's pressing, conscience-pricking social problems, such as alcoholism, medicare, premarital sex, or racial discrimination. Not one has given any comfort or hope for tomorrow in this nuclear age. Not one has taken us to task for failing to live up to the Christian teachings of brotherhood and love. The ministers have preached in circles, in platitudes, and in clichés. There were no strong signposts put up for the way ahead. Sermons preached on old Biblical texts and stories not related to today's troubled times are obscure and meaningless.

"I found it troubling that children are small shadows who slip quietly into pews and just as quietly fidget, kneel, and grope in complicated prayer books. At a given signal, they file out uninterestedly in an untidy, straggling procession behind a young altar-boy bearing a cross. No one ever acknowledged their presence in the service and yet, in many cases, when the children left, the pews were sparsely occupied. I attended only one children's service; it was disappointingly geared to a mentality far below that of our knowledgeable children of today.

"The services I attended would have been unbearably flat without the relief of choir music. Hymn-singing, however, might as well be dispensed with. Hardly any of the congregation made any attempts at all to sing the tuneless dirges that are supposed to reflect Christian joy and love. With some humorous satisfaction, I noticed that the morning I attended a church service that was being broadcast on the radio, the processional and opening hymns were well-known old favourites, and the singing was strong and lively.

"My Sunday morning subway rides and church attendance convinced me that if women were not churchgoers, there would be no church. They far outnumber the men. Perhaps women are naturally more religious, but I felt strongly that going to church was an "outing" for those women tied in all week, for the lonely women for whom the interminable length of Sunday is almost unbearable, and for those who like to get dressed up in their Sunday best. In all fairness I must say that there is no doubt in my mind that church has always been a meeting and a gathering place for lonely people.

"What *did* I find of value in the church service? I must admit that the participation of the congregation in the Communion Service was the most moving and eloquent part of the ones I attended. Perhaps, after all, this is the only real and vital need of a true Christian."

3   THE LUKEWARM PULPIT

THAT MANY SERMONS of today tend to be spiritless, irrelevant, dull, and badly delivered, there can be little doubt. Almost all the sermons my observer took down in shorthand could have been preached with scarcely a comma changed a century ago. Some ministers may wonder what is so wrong with that since the Christian message is itself eternal. But surely eternal messages ought to be expressed in contemporary idioms and with contemporary techniques if they are to be understood. On several occasions, when I asked my observer to condense her weekly shorthand notes and give me the gist of what a sermon was about, she found she could not do it; she had no idea what it was the man in the pulpit was trying to get across. Of all the sermons she listened to, only one made any reference to a subject that was topically contentious. Ironically the subject dealt with the controversy within the church concerning the invitation extended to me to prepare this book. Although she listened carefully and made near-verbatim notes, my observer was unable to discover which side of the controversy the preacher was on. Nor, on reading her notes, was I.

If the congregation is made restless or sleepy by the modern sermon, it is not only because the message is obscured through the use of an archaic terminology, or because clergymen preach by rote—"like actors who have learned their lines," in Mumford's phrase. It is also because the message itself, apart from its language and its method of delivery, is irrelevant and weak. It is a saying among ecclesiastics that most ministers preach to the right of their theology, that they are more conservative in the pulpit than they are in the parlour. Many a man known to be liberal in his own philosophic approach to Christianity may sound like a mossback when he preaches; often enough, because church elders are elderly in attitude as well as age, he will purposely clothe his ideas in an ancient terminology. In doing so he waters down and obscures a message that, delivered honestly, forthrightly, and in simple language, could electrify his congregation. The fact is that most ministers do not want to electrify or disturb anybody, and that is why so many preachers have lost their power.

"You just don't say what you believe from the pulpit," one Anglican priest told me recently. I have heard this remark echoed in various ways from many clergymen. As a result, the preacher has long since lost his ability to convince or change people by the power of his words or the conviction of his message. Churchgoers are not fools, and they are not really impressed by men who mouth the same hackneyed phrases Sunday after Sunday. "You know damn well what the clergyman says isn't what people believe or think," one cleric said to another in my presence during a discussion on this subject.

The classic anthropological and sociological studies on typical communities on both sides of the Atlantic point up the lack of topicality in the Sunday sermon. In their two visits to Middletown, ten years apart, the Lynds found no appreciable difference in sermon topics: "To such controversial issues as internationalism, disarmament, pacifism, labor organization, social planning . . . civil liberty, the amendment of the Constitution, socialized medicine and birth control, the great majority of the churches of Middletown present the negative face of the community, or are silent, or talk in such generalities their position is equivocal." [13] The mass-observation studies of Worktown in England reported, similarly, that no effort was being made in the pulpits to tackle specifically modern problems or to keep in touch with the swirl of contemporary life. References to current affairs were rare: "Vague goodness is felt to be enough and will bring its own rewards. . . . This absence of topicality was a noticeable feature of most sermons heard during 1937 and 1960. . . ." [14]

When the Anglican Church of Canada in 1964 took, at my suggestion, a careful poll of 248 of its ministers to discover how relevant their sermons were to everyday life, the results indicated that the situation in Canada is not very different.

Of 240 ministers who replied to the question "Would you say that you chose your sermon topics from the front pages of the newspaper?" sixty-two per cent answered "rarely" or "never"; thirty-five per cent answered "occasionally"; three per cent answered "fairly often"; none answered "regularly."

As a check against this question, the ministers were also asked whether they had preached or made reference during the last six months to specific topical subjects in the secular world. These topics were: the racial problem in South Africa, the southern United States, Canada and elsewhere; capital punishment; prison reform; a national health scheme; businessmen's morals; the population explosion; birth control; homosexuality; a specific topical aspect of the Cold War; the Cuban crisis; the nuclear problem; and the then-current controversy over the CBC's telecasting at Easter of the program "The Open Grave." * Only sixty-eight min-

---

* *The Open Grave* was a televised play on the Canadian Broadcasting Corporation's national network that dealt with the Easter story, at Eastertime, in modern terms. The play took the form of a simulated live telecast from Toronto's Mount Pleasant Cemetery with studio cut-ins purporting to report on the mysterious disappearance, from his grave, of a recently executed religious leader. Before the play was telecast several church leaders, including the Anglican Bishop of Toronto, denounced it sight unseen as blasphemous.

isters of the 248 who responded—about twenty-seven per cent—
had preached sermons on any of these subjects. One hundred and
thirty-seven—a little over half—had made some passing reference
during the course of a sermon to one or more of the topics. By
contrast, 181—over seventy per cent—had preached, at least once,
on the subject of church unity.

The comments that accompanied the return of these question-
naires were often enlightening: "Most headlines are about ephem-
eral matters. . . . I don't subscribe to the local paper. . . . What
has the newspaper to say to a generation that stands in need of
conversion? . . . One cannot be sure of newspaper reports. . . .
'Newsy' sermons prevent long-range planning. . . . We preach
only from the Bible." Is it any wonder, then, that the people who
sit through today's sermons have ceased to blow hot or cold?

Let it be remembered that the founder of the Christian faith
was a master of contemporary communication. The stories that
he told sprang directly from the lives of the people to whom he
spoke, for they dealt with such things as the sowing of grain, the
tending of sheep, and the netting of fish. In every phrase he uttered, there was a feeling of immediacy and identification. But it
was a totally different kind of world from the one we know today.
The parables of Jesus were directed specifically to a semi-tropical
desert-nation of herdsmen, peasants, and fisherfolk, many of them
slaves, all of them living under the yoke of a military conqueror
whom they had no hope of overthrowing. It was a world in which
the tax collector was a pariah, the Samaritan a despised enemy,
the leper a familiar sight, the ragged beggar a fact of life. It was
a far cry from the sophisticated, affluent, business-dominated
democracy of our time.

Where are the modern parables to fit the New Age? One rarely
hears them from the pulpit, though one occasionally reads them
in the newspapers, which seem sometimes to have usurped the
function of the pulpit. The men in the pulpit seem content to re-
tell the ancient stories, so many of which make no impact on a
modern congregation. The story of the Good Samaritan, to take a
single example, loses much of its point today, since it is difficult to
make a modern audience understand how the people of Christ's
time felt about Samaritans. A story about a Good German, told

during World War II or perhaps about a Good Communist or a Good Homosexual or, in certain parts of the world, a Good Negro, might have considerably more effect.

As part of my preparation for writing this book, I engaged in a series of discussions with various Anglican ministers once a week for a period of some months. Again and again we kept returning to this matter of the sermon, and again and again I was interested to discover that the priests who talked with me, and often agreed with what I had to say about the irrelevancy of the modern pulpit, tried to convince me that sermons really did not matter that much, since sermons were only a small part of overall church work. As one of them put it: "I question how far the pulpit can be accepted as an image. I'd suggest that a change in the pulpit is perhaps of the least significance in the coming revolution. After all, the centre of the church is not the pulpit, unless you use the word 'pulpit' to describe the whole posture of the ordained ministry."

This may well be true in theory; but the lay public does not understand it. To the average man, the real image of the Church emerges from the Sunday sermon. And why not? It is the one portion of an otherwise ritualized service that changes from Sunday to Sunday. Prayers, hymns, and lesson readings all come out of printed books. But the sermon allows the priest a personal moment of communication with his flock. As the Lynds discovered in Middletown, the sermons "forming the focus of the religious life of Protestant adults . . . are the chief means of diffusing habits of thought and action approved by the church to its members." [15] From the sermon each Sunday, the people learn what the Church has to say to them, or perhaps what it *has not* to say. If the sermon is timid, if its message is irrelevant or obscure, if the views it espouses are obviously safe ones, if its style is fuzzy or hackneyed, then the Church's image will surely suffer as it has indeed suffered.

The lukewarm pulpit makes hypocrites of its occupants. The priest who says less than he believes from the pulpit, the priest who says merely what he thinks people want him to say, the priest who pulls his punches because the religious establishment requires it, loses a portion of his dignity. He knows it and so does his congregation; hypocrisy is not so easy to conceal. And it is this that is bothering many of the men who serve the Church today. I found it intriguing, during my discussions about the pulpit and its image, to note that I had struck a sensitive nerve among those who were present; again and again we returned to this subject; again and again many of those in the room tried to minimize the matter, until it became clear that the whole problem of the Sunday sermon and its lack of conviction is one that profoundly worries men of conviction. No wonder then that some, in desperation, have seriously suggested a moratorium on all preaching.

4   THE REJECTION OF TWENTIETH-CENTURY MEDIA

ONE CAN with validity ask, however, whether the Church has seriously considered some of the modern alternatives to the local minister preaching twice each Sunday from his pulpit to a smattering of inattentive listeners. In an electronic age is this really the best we can do? The church service is a form of theatre and was so recognized in past centuries; with all that we know about theatre today as a means of education and communication, is it not possible to suggest some improvements?

It is not in the cards that every ordained man should be, or indeed need be, a powerful public speaker or pulpit personality. Yet there are in the Church some men whose value lies in their ability to stir souls, rekindle emotions, and communicate eternal truths in a fresh, relevant, and compelling manner. Why should such men be confined to a single church or a single congregation? If doctors, advertising men, business tycoons, and even schools can use closed-circuit television to reach hundreds of thousands of people who would not otherwise receive the message, why should the Church not be using it too, to bring its most inspired spokesmen to the attenion of larger numbers of churchgoers?

Why, on certain Sundays, could not a flick of the switch in a small parish church bring in a guest sermon from several thousand miles away?

Why, indeed, in an age when new techniques of communication are constantly being studied and perfected, cannot the word "sermon" be more broadly interpreted than it was when all messages were delivered by one man speaking directly to another? I have never been able to understand why so many churches seem so loath to bring the congregation into active participation with the priest during the sermon period. Why should not members of the congregation ask questions? Indeed, why cannot any man stand up in church and argue with his pastor? What is wrong with controlled discussions, debates, panels, and seminars?

Must a sermon be nothing more than a speech which one man delivers and others passively accept? Why, for instance, cannot a sermon be a play, as it sometimes was in the Middle Ages? With all our knowledge and mastery of theatrical, television, and motion-picture techniques, is it not possible to produce on tape or on film or on closed circuits modern morality plays that could, on certain occasions, replace the sermon?*

The great teachers have always communicated through symbols, and there is nothing very new about that particular technique. But the modern Church is desperately in need of some contemporary symbols to make the impact of its message felt. I find nothing untoward in Peter Berger's suggestion that, in place of a cross on the altar, some churches should try the experiment of substituting an electric chair—and the figure in that chair might easily be that of a Negro. Yet any attempt to modernize the symbolism of the Christian message is likely to cause an outcry from the eleders of the religious establishment, as a much-publicized incident in the spring of 1964 made clear.

One of the worst blows suffered by the Anglican Church in Canada was the ill-advised attack made by the Bishop of Toronto and others on the attempt of a cbc-television producer to render

* The nearest approach to this concept has been that of the Christian Drama Council of Canada and its acting arm, The Company of Pilgrims, whose productions have been used in certain churches in some Ontario cities as part of the service in place of the sermon.

the Easter message in contemporary terms. Whether or not the play "The Open Grave" was a success is really beside the point. It was an honest and sincere endeavour by a group of laymen to do what the Church should have been doing years ago: using modern electronic devices and modern communication techniques to breathe fresh vitality into a message that has lost much of its sting through familiarity. To damn this in advance as blasphemous and sacrilegious, without even seeing it first, was itself damnable. By doing so the church leaders served notice on an already skeptical community that they were just as out-of-date, timid, and fearful of change as their atheistic critics had been charging.

The failure of the Church to make any sensible or imaginative use of television is in itself a terrible indictment. If ever a medium was ready-made to carry the Christian message, this one was. Yet those few clerics who do occasionally make use of television do not really understand the medium, while the Church as a whole simply ignores it. Indeed it is doubtful that the Church understands the modern science of communication at all, or that the Church realizes it *is* a science and not a hit-or-miss proposition, that it ought to be devoting some of its best minds to the understanding of that science, and that it probably ought to be incorporating in the curricula of its divinity schools a course on the specific techniques of modern communicating.

The twentieth century marks the first time in the Church's long history that it has lost control of *all* the contemporary means of communication. There was a time when the reverse was true; the Church was totally in control. In the Dark Ages, the priests were almost the only ones who could write. Until Shakespeare's time the Church controlled the theatre. Until the late Renaissance, it was in full charge of sculpture and painting. In Bach's day and later it controlled most music. In the nineteenth century, in a thousand towns and villages, it was the Church, through its ownership of the public halls, that held sway over the Big Meeting, the chief mode of expression at the time.

But in the twentieth century, the Church's attitude to the new electronic media is one of distrust. There seems to be a feeling that all twentieth-century media are somehow indecent. In the words of Mavor Moore, the Canadian producer who helped to set up the first television network in Canada, "The ministers of the Church not only demonstrate an abysmal lack of knowledge of the medium, they really don't want to soil their hands in it; they don't want to adapt old methods of communication to new techniques."

Moore had considerable experience with this attitude in the early days of Canadian television. Much of it, he recalls, was entirely negative: "I remember one visit I had from a United Church minister who was preparing a resolution, part of which was to state that there should be no scenes whatsoever on television showing people drinking or referring to people drinking. I pointed out to him that this would prevent us from televising most of Shakespeare and a good deal of the Bible. The resolution was withdrawn."

Moore adds that most ministers with whom he dealt—and he feels that this still applies to the Religious Advisory Council which passes on all religious programs shown on Canadian television—"had the rather naïve idea that the more 'church programs' there were on television, the further ahead they'd be. There was no appreciation at all of the fact that people can easily turn off their sets or switch to another channel."

By "church programs," the ministers involved with television really meant telecasts of church services or sermons. "They were totally disinclined to approve any exciting examinations of religion," Moore says. "I remember once asking whether or not it would be possible to put an atheist on television. I was told there was no possibility whatsoever. But it seemed to me then, as it does now, that unless you deal with the sinews of religion, unless you're able through discussion and debate to meet the doubts expressed by the average man in an exciting and compelling fashion, then from the point of view of religious programming you're doomed."

The truth is that the Church has failed to come to grips with television, which it continues to treat and to think of in old-fashioned terms. To most churchmen, TV is just another means to communicate what used to be communicated in other ways. Superimposed on this fallacy is the general suspicion that television is something "bad," a snobbery that has its genesis in the same kind of attitude that once banned the African drums and nose flutes as pagan. The Church has yet to discover that television is neither good nor bad; it is there. It is, as Marshall McLuhan has been saying for some time, more than a medium of expression; it is one of the great facts of the New Age.[16] It is part of us, and it is changing us. To survive, the Church must master it.*

Having done that, of course, the Church must still learn to speak with conviction and with courage. The answer to Karl Barth's question "Why don't you force us to pay attention?" is that the Church is afraid—afraid not only to speak out in Christian terms about the issues relevant to our time, but afraid also to try anything new, to experiment, to investigate the changes in the world that have brought changes in the means of speaking out. It is as if the religious establishment hesitates to break new ground, for fear its own position may be undermined.

At the time of the controversy over "The Open Grave," a Baptist clergyman, the Reverand Wade Jumper, who is an expert on the synthesis of religion and psychology, put his finger on some of the Church's secret fears:

Dramatically . . . the producers . . . have now asked the church why is it sacred for you to interpret the life of Jesus; but sacrilegious for us? And they have flung down the gauntlet by bringing a modernized Resurrection before the public via television. . . . The church has been revealed more clearly than ever as being in poor emotional health. Her state is one of unrest and anxiety. . . . Consider the overtone of nervous suspicion throughout; emotion-packed accusations such as "offensive," "sacrilegious," and "blasphemous"; add to this irrational pre-judgments pronounced by eminent church spokesmen usually noted for their calm and sympathetic approach to problems. Were these earmarks of fearful anxiety in the church detected in an individual, the most conservative analyst or psychologist would consider the subject deeply insecure. Nothing less can be said about the church—the church is insecure and

---

* It was not until 1961 that the Anglican Church, following the lead of the United Church of Canada, set aside a small budget for broadcasting. This has resulted in the *Checkpoint* radio series and the *Comment and Conviction* television series, both critically successful, though many stations seem unwilling to give them the time slots they deserve.

afraid! The church fears the loss of her exalted position. She deems her position to depend upon control—control of interpretation over the life of Jesus. The church refuses to share the interpretative role with secular pursuits for fear that revered religious truths will lose their sacred meaning. Their loss of sacred meaning will mean her loss of control. Her intense reaction to "The Open Grave" symbolizes a desperate possessiveness prompted by fear—fear of dethronement.[17]

Once again we return to the problem of the religious establishment's preoccupation with its institutional entity, the continued missionary emphasis on its "absolute rightness," its obsessive attempts to preserve certain jargons, myths, and mysteries in the belief that by so doing it will also preserve itself. And, of course, it *will* preserve itself, as a fly is preserved in amber, or a corpse in glacial ice, or a fossil embedded in imperishable granite.

5 FAITH WITHOUT DOGMA

FROM A LAYMAN'S POINT OF VIEW, at least, the most startling and controversial book to be issued by a churchman in recent years has been *Honest to God* by John A. T. Robinson, Bishop of Woolwich. Some seven-hundred thousand copies of this attractive and inexpensive paperback edition have already been printed.

The Bishop's thesis is not a difficult one to understand, though some of his detail is fairly hard going. Drawing heavily on three German philosopher-theologians, Rudolph Bultmann, Paul Tillich, and the martyred Dietrich Bonhoeffer (they are not always themselves in agreement), Robinson says that twentieth-century man can no longer be treated as a child who needs to believe in charming fairy tales in order to understand eternal truths. A world "come of age" has already rejected the concept of a white-bearded Big Daddy perched on a cloud. It is in the process of also rejecting the Mysterious Friendly Spirit somewhere "out there" in space.

We need, says Robinson, a new concept of what God is; we need a God who is less remote, a God who is "the ultimate depth of all our being, the creative ground and meaning of all our existence." [18]

The day is swiftly coming, says Robinson, when the traditional image of God will be as remote from modern man as the Hellenic deities on Olympus. If Christianity is to survive, it must, to use Bultmann's word, "demythologize." Unless it cuts itself free of the clinging undergrowth of myth, it will be strangled. Robinson does not say that myths should be abandoned; after all we continue to learn from the Greek myths, and it is not necessary to believe that Oedipus really lived to understand the sin of pride that brought him low. But he does believe it is important that certain Biblical tales be recognized as myths, and *then* used to illuminate certain truths. For it is on this aspect of the Christian religion—the stubborn confusion of myth with history—that the most telling of the atheists' attacks are centred.

The reaction to *Honest to God* has been as electrifying, as intriguing, and as surprising as the book itself. I have already mentioned one response: the feeling among many of the clergy that it is a dangerous tract to place in the hands of untutored laymen. Two other church reactions are interesting. One has been that the Bishop has come perilously close to blasphemy, that he is probably not a Christian, but an atheist or agnostic, and that the book borders on heresy. The Archbishop of Canterbury is one who has inclined towards this general view. The other reaction has been quite the opposite: that the Bishop is not really saying anything new—that, in the words of H. E. W. Turner, Professor of Divinity at the University of Durham, much of it is "old stuff by now," [19] and that the Bishop's general thesis has long been held by theologians.

If it is old stuff, then why all the fuss? Why have hundreds of thousands of people bought the book? Why has the Bishop been attacked by some clerics, praised by others? Why is his post-box jammed with letters from thousands of people who have told him that he has let a breath of fresh air into their lives? Why is *Honest to God* the only theological book that has got through to the mass public in modern times? Is it possibly because, in the Bishop's own words, "many popular religious ideas are still incredibly more naïve than bishops or clergy often suppose"? Is it because what is "old stuff" to some sophisticated theologians is electrifyingly new to the masses with whom the theologians cannot communicate? Is it because the men in the pulpit are reluctant to say aloud what is in their hearts and what, in fact, they do say among themselves? Is it because it is simply easier, less troublesome, and less disturbing to take the Biblical stories at their face value and transmit them to the congregation without too much modern interpretation or comment?

The impact of the book on the Anglican clergy of Canada can be discerned from several questions in the Church's 1964 survey of its priests. In the sample of 248 respondents, 164 had read the whole book and another eighteen had read part of it. Of this group, seventy-three agreed with it in the main (sixty-five of these reported having "some reservations"), sixty-three agreed and disagreed in about equal measure, twenty-eight disagreed with some reservations, and only six disagreed whole-heartedly. (A few did not answer all the questions, hence the arithmetical discrepancy.) Significantly, of those who had read the book through, a huge majority—slightly more than eighty per cent—thought it was beneficial.

If *Honest to God* has done nothing else, it has pointed out to the Church the great hunger that its communicants have for a reinterpretation of the Biblical tales. For the past century, men of conscience and imagination have been wrestling with themselves over what appears to be a conflict between the Bible and science. In the space age, blind faith in dogma is not enough. Modern man has been taught to question, to probe, to weigh pieces of evidence rationally; a church that insists he accept certain tales and certain ideas without question or argument cannot hold his respect.

It is instructive to remember that, in matters of Old Testament mythology, the Church has undergone, in the past century, a radical shift. When, in 1860, the authors of a book called *Essays and Reviews* dared to question the theory of eternal damnation, and suggest that the story of Adam and Eve was not literally true, they were attacked as atheists and heretics. Such things are no longer matters of contention in the major churches, though some

Baptists, in 1964, objected violently when their church accepted Sunday School material that made the same point.

It is now possible to have faith in the truths that Genesis teaches without believing that some few thousand years ago the world was created in six days, or that a woman named Eve, constructed from the rib of a man named Adam, mothered the human species. Yet even today some churchmen are reluctant to come to grips with the Genesis legends. I was astonished, while preparing this book, to hear an Anglican clergyman I respect, the rector of a large middle-class suburban parish, state that he accepted the Adam and Eve story as told because it was "as good an explanation as any—just as good a theory as the theory of evolution, which has never been proved."

In any contest between Biblical history and scientific inquiry, Biblical history is bound to lose, as it has been losing all through the ages since the time of Copernicus. As Bishop Robinson has pointed out, it has been "essential to the defense of Christian truth to recognize and assert that these stories were *not* history and therefore not in competition with the alternatives of anthropology or cosmology." [20] To suggest that they are is to play into the hands of the Church's critics.

It was the Darwinian controversy that forced theologians to clarify their own thinking on the mythological aspects of Genesis; their ability to do so undoubtedly saved Christianity in a scientific age. Modern scientific man could not believe in the literal truth of many of the Old Testament tales, which is not to say that he could not believe in their meaning and relevance. He could understand the inherent truths which certain myths dramatize. Indeed, it can be argued that myths, recognized as myths, become more profound and significant as teaching aids than if one is forced to struggle with them as literal happenings.

The time has already arrived when the New Testament stories must also be subjected to the same scrutiny. These must include the various miraculous events that are said to have attended Christ's birth, his ministry, and his death. There is already, for instance, a division of opinion within the Anglican Church about the Apostle's Creed with its emphasis on the virgin birth. Is it

necessary to believe literally in every word of the Creed in order
to be a Christian? Many clerics would insist on it. Others would
tend to agree with Bishop James Pike of California that the Creed
ought to be treated as a hymn, and sung in the way that people
sing the National Anthem, without specific regard to the words,
but with a sort of emotion that recalls one's origins. "There are
several phrases in the creed that I cannot affirm as literal prose
sentences," Pike has written. "But I can certainly sing them as a
kind of war song picturing major convictions in poetic terms." [21]

The passions that this and attendant arguments arouse can be
likened to those that flamed around the Adam and Eve myth a
century ago. The Methodist Church in Great Britain recently expelled as a heretic one of its ministers who denied the virgin birth.
When the sample of Anglican priests was asked, "Do you believe
in the literal truth of the Apostle's Creed?" 152 of 248—some
sixty-two per cent—replied, "Yes—fully." Another sixty-two,
however—twenty-five per cent—answered they believed in most
but not all of it; six said they believed in part of it; nine gave a flat
"No," and seventeen did not answer the question.

The comments of some of the total believers were impassioned:
"The very fact that you feel the need to ask this question speaks
volumes about the state of the Canadian clergy. . . ." "Yes, I
would hardly stand up in church and lead my people in reciting it
if I did not. . . ." "Good God—yes! How can I stay in the priesthood if I don't believe the Church's formula of the Faith? . . ."
"That is why I was ordained as a priest. . . ."

There were others, however, who questioned the use of the
word "literal," which they found ambiguous, "too loaded a word,"
as one put it. "If 'literal' means without mysticism or metaphor,
then no. Where is Hell?" commented another. "Certainly I believe
in the Divinity of Jesus Christ, but I do not probably embody in
the word 'divinity' the same meaning that I had twenty years
ago," wrote a third. There were some who suggested that the
Creed needed interpretation and a more modern idiom. Many said
they believed in it fully, but not in the narrow sense, with reference to words and phrases like "ascend," "descend," "sitteth on
the right hand," and so on. It is these terms, of course, with their
emphasis on a three-layer universe and an anthropomorphic God,

that maintain the image of a deity that Bishop Robinson and others consider irrelevant to a scientific world.

The argument over the virgin birth has been joined for some time and has, for some time, been a subject of contention in the church pages of the daily newspapers. We can all agree that the birth of Christ was an event unique in history, but must every man be required to believe in certain specific mechanics of that birth, before he can be called a Christian? Many Christian leaders insist upon it, and therein, it seems to me, lies a grave danger to Christianity as a whole. George Bowman, the editor of the *Baptist News,* has unwittingly mapped out the pitfalls when he writes: "If you deny the virgin birth then Christianity is without foundation because the Bible ceases to be the authoritative criterion by which to judge all statements for or against Chritsianity." [22]

But must Chritsianity be required to stand or fall on a minor question of mechanics? "The deepest truths," says Bishop Robinson, "are like butterflies. If you try to pin them down, you kill them." [23] To call a man an atheist because he does not believe in the virgin birth or the miracle of the loaves and fishes or the raising of Lazarus is to throw the baby out with the bathwater. Tillich's broader definition of atheism better fits the New Age. To him, the real atheist is the man who can truly say: "Life has no depth! Life is shadow. Being itself is surface only. If you could say this in complete seriousness you would be an atheist; but otherwise you are not. He who knows about depth knows about God." [24]

In an age that has been taught the need for asking questions, there are going to have to be legitimate areas of agnosticism within the faith. The fact that the Bishop of Woolwich dared to say he did *not* know the answer to certain things was what appealed to thousands. To them his book came as a fresh wind blowing through the stale air of smug and absolute certainty that has characterized the fossilized Church. As Bonhoeffer wrote, not long before his death, it is "wrong to use God as a stopgap for the incompleteness of our knowledge." [25]

The question that the Church must now come to grips with is this: "Is it possible to have faith without dogma?" I should think the answer would be in the affirmative. More, I should think that in the late twentieth century it would be almost impossible to have faith *with* dogma; for only by facing up to the unknowable, and admitting honestly to the presence of the unknowable, can religion make its peace with science.

It is hardly a secret that, because of its reliance on dogma, Christianity has accepted an unscientific attitude to life. By this I mean that anyone who really uses his mind finds himself having serious trouble relating the contribution of modern secular thinkers to his whole religious philosophy. He finds himself face to face with several dilemmas. His primitive religious beliefs, the simple beliefs instilled in him at Sunday School and church, become subject to the attack of a growing and maturing intellect.

Thus he faces a number of choices. He can accommodate himself to the problem, and thus lose the vitality of his beliefs. He can simply quit thinking, which is what a lot of clergymen seem to me to have done. He can compartmentalize his mind, as did the army chaplains surveyed by Waldo Burchard. Or he can find himself facing the dilemma of the honest man. The honest man hesitates to be dogmatic, and for that reason often seems to be weak; certainly this is true within the Church, where the dogmatic personality appears so much stronger than the one that equivocates through thought. (The authors of *The Authoritarian Personality* discovered a correlation between racial prejudice and those who felt dogmatically that people should have "complete faith in some supernatural force." [26]) The man who thinks, who searches, and who questions understands what the novelist undertsands: that the world is fairly free of blacks and whites. Even the scientist realizes that he cannot be too positive about anything, since today's scientific truth may have to be adapted, augmented, or amended by tomorrow's discoveries. He once believed in solids and masses which now, he discovers, are made up largely of empty space occupied by minute whirling electrons that are little more than wriggles of energy.

If the scientist looking at the history of science resolves to keep an open mind, so surely must the clergyman who studies the history of science and religion. For when dogmas are shattered by scientific evidence, the faith as a whole is shaken. No one can deny, for example, the serious impact that modern psychiatry has made on the Church. It has seriously bruised, if it has not destroyed, the idea that man is responsible for his own actions. If a man is not entirely responsible for what he does, if he acts in a certain manner because of parental influence or environmental background, if he has compulsions to do things that are "wrong" because he has no choice within his own psyche, how can he be held responsible before his God? How can all the complicated forces within a behavioural cycle be lumped together and simplified under the single word "sin"? How, in short, can the Church in the New Age perpetuate dogma?

Why, in the New Age, is dogma necessary at all? What is wrong with a man—be he layman or priest—saying honestly: "I don't know"? What is wrong with reverent agnosticism with the emphasis on the word "reverent"? What is wrong with a clergyman saying in all Christian humility: "Because of the limitations of my mind and the nature of the subject, I cannot know the final answer"?

The Church itself has moved a considerable distance from the grandiose pretensions of absolute rightness that once allowed it to describe the shape and nature of heaven and the features of the Almighty in specific terms. Now about these areas the Church itself says: "We cannot know." What is wrong with the Church frankly admitting that there are many more specific things that it cannot know, but that there are some other things that it does believe: that it believes, for instance, truth is better than a lie, honesty better than a deceit, love and mercy better than hate and mistrust—that it believes in the general principles laid down by its founder and demonstrated by influential Christians across the ages.

What does this do to faith? If one's faith is in Christ, and not in dogma, how can that faith be harmed? Dogma is, after all, only what Christians formulate as a result of their observation of Christ and the action of their lives. The most rational of men still live to a large extent by faith, whether they are Christians or not. Men have faith in their own existence, faith in the love of their wives and children, faith that there will continue to be a highway on the other side of an unknown hill, faith that they will live to rise again on the morrow. We believe in many things, with no certain knowledge that they are true; but we do know that certain kinds of faith, acted upon, achieve results.

Surely, then, the ultimate faith of the committed Christian is not faith in an inviolate dogma but faith in a God about whom that dogma speaks. For more and more men, the acceptance of the Christian faith in the New Age will become possible only when they discover, as John Wren-Lewis discovered, that they do not need to accept a whole body of specific beliefs which they consider superstitious and once rejected wholesale.

I have always found it interesting that the religious establishment, in its attacks on communism, often strikes at those very qualities in that foreign faith that parallel those of institutional Christendom: the enslavement by Communist "priests" of free and uncommitted minds; the dogmatic insistence on the absolute rightness of the Communist cause; the insistence on unswerving belief without question or argument. This is straight religious fanaticism, and we who call ourselves free rightly abhor it. The Church, then, does its own followers the same disservice when it forces them to cling to an equally rigid orthodoxy.

"My concern," says Bishop Robinson, "is precisely not to throw out the myths, but to enable us to use them." [27] He rightly sees that to do so we must understand the difference between myth and history. A slavish dependence on one particular, inflexible mythology threatens the continued existence of the Church, since that mythology is "in peril of becoming a source of incredulity rather than an aid to faith." [28]

The Church can no longer communicate with modern man by pretending to the literal truth of Biblical tales; it can, however, more clearly communicate if it undertsands the deeper truths that these stories have to tell. In this area of communication, as in so many others, the Church must cease relying on absolutes and adopt a more flexible attitude; for unless it makes of its myths and legends a useful tool, and not a barrier to understanding, all communication will shortly cease.

𝕯 THE FUTURE

IS REVOLUTION POSSIBLE?

THE THESIS OF THIS BOOK is that the Christian philosophy and ethic has been shackled by its institutional chains; that "religion," as we know it today in all its organizational manifestations, is something quite different from the Christianity of Galilee; that it tends to attract a different kind of person from the kind that followed the original precepts; that, in its desperate effort to preserve its established entity, the Church has become fossilized; and that this fossilization has prevented it from moving with the world.

It is the thesis of this book that a violent revolution—violent in the psychological and social rather than the physical sense—is needed to save Christianity. Others, far more competent than I, have sensed a coming upheaval. The Bishop of Woolwich, who has become unwittingly and perhaps unwillingly the spokesman for the inarticulate within the Church, sees the need for a "radically new mold and metamorphosis of Christian belief and practice";[1] without that kind of revolution, he believes the Christian religion will come to be abandoned. His book sparked some similar opinions; the Canon Theologian of New York's Cathedral of St. John the Divine says "we are simply in the midst of a theological Copernican revolution. We had best adjust ourselves to it."[2] Several have echoed Bonhoeffer's words about the coming of age of the world. The Dean of St. Paul's says it is time for the Church to "put away childish things."[3] The *Guardian*'s religious writer, Monica Furlong, refers to "a new mutation of Christian, who is

willing and eager to question every item of his faith, who is bored
to death with the old clichés, the old humbug and the great herd
of sacred cows, and who believes that to disable either his mind or
his senses is to dishonour Christ." [4]

All these people seem fairly confident that the revolution is
on its way; and certainly there are signs that the churches are
changing. Both the United and the Anglican churches in Canada
are engaged in the kind of public soul-searching that was so evident at the Congress in 1963. Both churches have demythologized
(to use Bultmann's term) their Sunday School texts, and the
United Church especially, through its Board of Evangelism and
Social Service, has been doing its best to place itself squarely in
the mainstream of social progress. (The Board sometimes en-
counters heavy going with the main body of the Church.) In
addition, Christian radicals in all the major churches—one must
not neglect here the Roman Catholics—are standing up to be
counted. When the Bishop of Toronto criticized "The Open
Grave," a vocal group of priests and laymen made it publicly clear
that the Church was not unanimously behind him.

To suggest that the Church's present form is its final one would,
to quote Mumford again, mean either "that the church was dead
or that Heaven had come upon the earth." [5] The Church, of course,
has constantly been changing since the time of St. Paul. Yester-
day's heresies have often enough become today's orthodoxies, and
the faith, though initially shaken, has managed to absorb the cool
Hellenistic philosophies, the humanism of the Renaissance and
the rationalism of Newtonian physics. Now it is struggling to
assimilate a whole new set of scientific ideas brought about by the
development in this century of the biological and social sciences.

But change has always been so slow as to seem imperceptible.
Catholicism defended mediæval cosmology for decades before it
dropped its opposition to the astronomers; Protestantism took
almost as long to come to terms with Darwin or to accept the idea
of birth control; it has yet to fully acknowledge Freud.

Until the nineteenth century, the Church was able, like a
majestic ship, to tack with leisurely dignity into the shifting
winds, and thus emphasize the apparent unchanging character of
essential religious beliefs. The modern Church has not reckoned

with the blinding acceleration of modern knowledge. Science moves like a space-craft at ever-increasing velocities, while the Church maintains its slow and stately progression. In a world attuned to sudden and continued change, the Church appears to fear it, believing no doubt that radical mutation will lower its institutional prestige. The truth is that its prestige has already been lowered because of its refusal to move with the times. With accelerated change in all other aspects of life, the Church's anachronistic position in modern society becomes more apparent. In Middletown, the churches appeared "to be forever bartering the opportunity for leadership in the area of change for the right to continue a shadowy leadership in the Changeless." [6] The leadership is indeed an illusory one. It is perhaps useful to remember that the Christian Church was born as the result of a revolution— and that, at the time, nothing less than a revolution would have done the trick.

This revolution was the result of action as much as talk, and it is in this area of action that the contemporary Church, especially the Protestant Church, is singularly weak. There is, within the social community, a growing skepticism about the Church, a feeling not only that it is all talk and no action, but also that it is all doubletalk based on *doublethink*. Dr. T. W. Adorno, the Director of the Institute of Social Research, has written of the United States that "the critique of religion as 'hypocritical' . . . is in this country as widespread as the Christian religion itself." [7]

I have already suggested that much of this attitude springs from the failure of the Sunday sermon to communicate the vitality of the Christian message in relevant contemporary terms. In the previous chapter, I made some tentative suggestions for improving the sermon, but the best immediate solution to this problem of communication might be to do as some churchmen have already suggested, to declare a moratorium on all pulpit-preaching for a period of at least a year and probably longer. This might allow some time and thought to be spent on non-pulpit sermons.

The best non-pulpit sermon that I know of was preached during the winter of 1963-64 by Father David Bauer, a Basilian Father. Father Bauer did not stand up before a congregation closeted behind stained-glass windows and talk in generalities about the need for honesty in everyday life or about the Christian values inherent in turning the other cheek. Father Bauer did no preaching at all. What he did was coach a Canadian Olympic hockey team and take it to Europe. It may be recalled that this Olympic hockey team was markedly different from some others that Canada had sent to the games, and that it set out, specifically, to be different.

First, this was an honest hockey team. The players were real amateurs, not fake amateurs; they were hand-picked by Father Bauer himself from the universities. No pseudo-amateurs or part-professionals were hidden in among the players. For the first time in years, Canada did not publicly lie about the men who played its national sport in world competition.

Second, the team and its coach made it clear by their actions that they intended to play cleanly in the Olympic tradition, and that they would eschew the kind of violence that, more and more, has come to characterize and brutalize professional profit-making sport in North America. They were determined to do this, even at the expense of winning. There was one remarkable and dramatic moment, when Father Bauer himself was struck by a stick thrown by an opposing player, Karl Oberg. Normally, this would have touched off a wild mêlée sparked by the kind of international recrimination that has been Canada's lot in past sports events overseas, but this time the coach held the players in check. He made a statement in which he said he was certain that the blow had been accidental and the next day took Oberg as his guest to the Russian-Czech game.

The team, of course, did its best to win. But the emphasis throughout was that methods were more important than goals, means counted more than ends, winning was secondary to the preservation of human dignity.

The team did not win. Yet, oddly, the sense of despair that is usually experienced on a national scale when a Canadian hockey squad goes down to defeat in Europe did not sweep the nation. Rather, there was a sense of pride in the fact that a truly honest amateur team had played cleanly and done its best, a pride deepened, perhaps, by the demonstrable fact that for the first time in years in Europe, Canadian hockey players were not villains in the eyes of the spectators—they were undeniably popular.

When I use the phrase "walking sermon," I think of Father Bauer preaching to the largest congregation in Canada—the readers of the newspaper sports pages—about the Christian way of life. If the adjective "preachy" has taken on unpleasant connotations, it is because few clergymen have either the imagination, the drive, or the opportunity to do what Father Bauer did. They are the prisoners of their pulpits. If Father Bauer had had a parish, could he have left it to go to Innsbruck? Would he have had time, between the endless home visits, the Women's Auxiliary sales, the Men's Club evenings, the ringing telephone, and the demands of two weekly sermons, to select an Olympic hockey team, much less coach one?

One of the strengths of the Roman Catholic Church is that so many of its priests are detached from parish work. This is not true of the Protestant denominations. Indeed, almost every ordained man, save those detached for hospital, university, or military chaplaincies, goes into the parochial structure. Of the 1,967 active Anglican clergymen in Canada, 1,786 are involved with parish work.

This perhaps helps explain the diversity between the "image" of the Roman Catholic and the Protestant clerics as portrayed in the stereotypes of Hollywood movies. The image of the Protestant is generally passive and often farcical. The image of the Catholic is generally active and always reverent. Since the days of Chaplin's two-reelers, we have seen in films a succession of comic curates and their tea-drinking wives. They have all too often been presented as bumbling do-gooders, pious moralists, "sissies," or faintly laughable and ineffectual figures. There have, of course, been exceptions. Protestant clergymen have also been presented as stern evangelists, enemies of demon rum and sin, preservers of local morals (in the narrow sense), and occasionally as decent and even courageous leaders. But, while the audience is often invited to laugh *at* the Protestant cleric, it laughs *with* the Catholic; Barry Fitzgerald may be a figure of humour, but he is never ridiculous. There are very few exceptions to the Catholic image of a two-fisted priest—a Hoodlum Priest running a half-way house for ex-convicts, a Boys' Town Priest rehabilitating delinquent youths, a Waterfront Priest fighting dishonesty in labour unions. The Fighting Father, usually Irish, has become a Hollywood folk hero. The wartime padre, who takes the men's part against the officers (more often, alas, in fiction than in fact) seems almost invariably to be a Roman Catholic.

Part of this image, unquestionably, is the result of the work of the considerable Roman Catholic lobby in the movie capital. But who can deny that the detached priests of the Catholic Church, with their dramatic living sermons, have immeasurably helped with the image-building? The Catholics scarcely need singing commercials produced by Stan Freberg to bolster their image; their best people do the job for them, and the Church has never been hesitant about making sure that the sermons they act out reach the widest possible audience.

Such men work in the tradition of Christ, Gandhi, Schweitzer, and Father Damien, which is to preach by *doing*. And it may be useful here to recall briefly Gandhi's method of solving the problem of communication in a land of three hundred and fifty million illiterates who lived in thousands of detached and isolated villages unreachable by radio.

Gandhi knew that he had to touch India to the quick, and that he had to touch it within a decade or two at the most. Words he could not use; he had to move his people by example. Thus he totally identified himself with the masses. He cast off his European garb and wore the simple *dhoti*, the peasant dress. He travelled on railways by third class, which is indescribable in Western terms. He ate little except nuts and curd, the food available to those without money. He slept on a mat on the floor and gave up all other privileges that would normally be his as a high-caste Hindu. Then, because he loved the people he served, he showed that he was prepared to die for them—to fast to death in order to get what he wanted for them. That these fasts were more than mere gimmicks was demonstrated to all when Gandhi, on more than one occasion, slipped into the coma that precedes death. It was obvious that he meant business. It was clear that what he was doing was for others, since he demonstrably asked nothing for himself.

In this fashion, the poorest and most illiterate Indian was shown—not told—that a man whom he had never met loved him more than he loved his own life. In this way Gandhi received, from millions of Indians who had no philosophical understanding of what he was trying to do and no comprehension of his political objectives, the same kind of total commitment that Gandhi's teacher, Christ, received from his followers two millennia before.

A similar lesson can be learned from a study of Alcoholics Anonymous. This organization has achieved, in a quarter of a century, more than the thousands of preachers who called down hell-fire on those who were slaves to demon rum. It succeeded where the preachers failed, because the men who formed the organization had been alcoholics themselves and so were trusted by those they helped, since it was obvious that they, too, had come through the hell-fire and damnation of chronic alcoholism. It is apparent to anyone who has come into contact with the AA that its members will put tnemselves to terrible personal inconvenience to help a fellow sufferer. They will leave the office, neglect family or business, climb out of bed in the dark of the night and travel long distances if they are called upon to do so. This total commitment is not lost upon those who ask for help.

It is not necessary to have a disease in order to cure it, but it is certainly obvious that an understanding of people is essential to the ministry. It is questionable, I think, whether the present sterile and antiseptic atmosphere in which many clergymen are raised allows them the kind of identification with the sinner or the outcast or the non-churchgoer so necessary to the kind of revolution the Church must undertake. Certainly the evidence of Dr. Feilding, already quoted about theological schools, suggests that the average divinity student does not have this identification. And certainly the suburban-parish atmosphere, with its emphasis on conformity and respectability, does not give it to him.

One of the questions that the Church, in its new mood of self-appraisal, should surely ask itself is this: Should we not have a cadre of "free lance" or independent priests—ordained men who, perhaps for a transitory period or perhaps for life, are detached from parish work, who have no base of operation, so that they can do those things that otherwise would not get done, because other priests are too busy with parish duties?

It is possible that the Church could demonstrate through such men the feasibility of living on faith. For if the Church really believes the gospels, what is wrong with saying to a specially selected group: "Go out and work for God; we make no promises; we give you no salary or material comforts; you are on your own." Those who believe that such a mission is doomed to failure or frustration might care to examine the record of the Reverend Morris Zeidman of Toronto, who for many years ran a soup kitchen for destitute men on precisely these terms.

The Church might even take a leaf from the Buddhist book and give such men begging bowls. Does someone whisper: "How demeaning!" But are not Christians supposed to understand and accept a life of humility?

There is an allied area which the Church may also wish to consider: the area of the worker-priest. Such experiments have been tried in Europe and have often met with opposition from the religious establishment. But what is essentially wrong with ordained men, perhaps still wearing the revered collar, going out into the world to take secular jobs? Why should not some priests be taxi-drivers? Or, to put it the right way around, why should not some taxi-drivers be priests? Why should not some assembly-line workers be priests? Why should not a television commentator or newspaper columnist be a priest? I have often thought the latter a useful occupation for certain members of the clergy; and I do not here mean the specifically religious column, but the kind that deals with the world, that does not "preach," but amuses as it instructs. It would be intriguing to see such a column appearing under the by-line of a man identified as an ordained minister. (It has always interested me to note that so many of the men who edit the religious pages of the great newspapers are laymen and quite often atheists.)

In short, why shouldn't a certain number of clergymen get

out into the world, at least for a time, not to talk but to act?* The advantage to the parish, when they finally return to it, seems to me to be self-evident; the advantage to Christianity, provided they act as Christians—as "walking sermons"—seems to me incalculable.

The objections that will be made are several. The main obstacle will be the kind raised by the bishop referred to earlier, who refused to ordain two young men as worker-priests because he had parishes without ministers. The Church, therefore, may be faced with this question: Which is more important in the long run in the times in which we live, the parish or the world? Must *all* ordained ministers busy themselves with "visits," with fundraising, with men's groups, women's auxiliaries, turkey dinners, and hollow sermonizing?

The question is perhaps a loaded one. And, I think, the choice is not really "either . . . or." The Church in considering this question might wish to consider a related one: Why is there such a shortage of clergymen today? Why are we having trouble getting men to wear the cloth? Why is it that we are attracting only a certain kind of man, the "passive-dependent" type mentioned previously?

One answer which is often given is that the present age does not offer the challenge to the priest that past ages did. It seems to me, however, that it is the Church and not the age that is to blame. To say that private industry and the other professions can outbid

---

* Again, it is important to remark on the exceptions within the church. The Reverend James Manly of the United Church, who operates out of a trailer-manse in the isolated pulp town of Port Alice on Vancouver Island, gave up parish visits in January 1964 to take a job as a clean-up man in the Pulp Machine Room. He did this for several reasons: "The fact that the town centred around the mill, my misgivings about being so dependent on the Board of Home Missions, the local congregation's struggle for finances, my dislike of visiting as the only way of getting to know people and my desire to be in touch with the men in the bunkhouses." Manly asks: "Is it good stewardship for small congregations to spend so much of their time and energy in raising money to support a full-time ministry that feels itself to be increasingly irrelevant?" His is not quite an isolated case. In Bralorne, British Columbia, the Reverend Sid Bowles, also of the United Church, works full time in the mines. In Toronto, the Reverend Don Heap has been working in industry for almost a decade.

the Church financially for the best men is to confuse the meaning of the term "best men." Surely the Church does not want men who are motivated solely by thoughts of material gain. But it is true that the social sciences have robbed the Church of some of its potential leaders, and many who might once have become ministers now become social workers, not always for financial reasons. It is often because the people involved believe they can accomplish more in the lay field than in the ministry.

It may be that one reason the Church does not get enough divinity students, and often gets the wrong kind, is that the Church has little to offer save parish life. It might be that, if the Church had something else to offer, something more dramatic, something that called for more dedication and sacrifice, something not tied to the materialistic suburban world, the Church might get a new kind of recruit, and it might get them in large numbers.

Such has been the experience of the Peace Corps in the United States. This call to sacrifice and commitment, with little material reward and much discomfort, has produced an astonishing response. The basic idea, of course, is based on Christian principles. The corps members are not to preach the religion of the American Way of Life. They are not to preach at all. They are not to live in the manner of many previous missionaries, both political and religious, in the compound on the hill; they are to exist at the same level as the underdeveloped peoples—as one of them. Their job is to help without comment; to be useful where they can be; to teach when asked, and to show. Their job, in brief, is to *act*, as selflessly as possible, in the hope that by their actions they will tell the world more about the United States than any number of Voice of America broadcasts. The pay in the Peace Corps is low, the terms of work tougher than any offered by modern labour unions or personnel departments. Yet the Peace Corps has had no trouble at all in recruiting more than the personnel it requires.

Is it not possible, then, that a new kind of ecclesiastical Peace Corps is needed? That a new kind of missionary is needed, not in far-off coral strands but at home? And is it not possible that the challenge may be so exciting that the Church will find no dearth of applicants?

There is at present a tentative movement toward this concept in the patterns of clinical-pastoral training that are developing in the United States. In the best American theological schools, students are required to work for one-quarter of the year in a hospital, mental home, or prison—exactly as an intern works. No Canadian theological school yet requires this. Some work is provided for at the local parish level, but often enough this is of very little use. There are many instances today in several English-speaking countries of top theological students who quit before being ordained, preferring to go out into the secular world. I am not suggesting that these men are lost to the Church; but their identification with the Church is lost, and in that sense the communication between the Church and the world is faulty.

It is clear that modern man is a different creature, mentally, psychologically, and socially, from Biblical man, mediæval man and, probably, Victorian man. The so-called "Modern Age," which replaced the Middle Ages at the dawn of the Renaissance, is the Modern Age no longer. Some new name will have to be found for the age that we have already entered and down whose corridors we are plunging at break-neck speed. In this book I have called it, simply, the New Age.

For this New Age we need a new kind of Church. The mentality of the New Age is secular, not religious, and any church that survives and flourishes and reaches the hearts and souls of men must be aware of this. Religion, if it was ever intended to be confined within four Gothic or baroque walls, certainly can no longer remain there. "A religion," says Yinger, in *Religion, Society and the Individual,* "will not hold the allegiance of a group of people who have acquired as a result of non-religious causes, new aesthetic tastes, new intellectual perspectives, new occupational interests, new moral conceptions—unless that religion adjusts to those changes." [8]

Religion as we know it, as distinct from Christianity, is, in my opinion, coming to an end, in spite of the present evidences of its power. And Christianity, if it is to survive as a meaningful faith and ethic, must rid itself of religion's trappings and false goals. It has been my observation that, just as many "religious" people are not really Christians, so many others, for whom Christianity is genuinely the clue to life and conduct, do not need or want what is called "religion" in the New Age. They reject it as Bonhoeffer rejected it, and it angers them that the establishment should require of them that they be "religious" before they can be called Christians.

If man has truly come of age, he no longer needs the father-figure of a God who, in Bishop Robinson's words, "must be 'there' to explain the universe, to protect him in his loneliness, to fill the gaps in his science, to provide the sanction for his morality." [9] We no longer need to cling to the daddy on the cloud; we need to revere the spirit within ourselves, and in the world around us, which represents ultimate reality, which gives a purpose to existence, which, to quote Paul Tillich, "is the ground of everything personal," which is bound up with "the feeling for the inexhaustible mystery of life, the grip of the ultimate meaning of existence and the invincible power of unconditional devotion." [10]

The Church then must embark on a long and perhaps painful examination of the kind of world in which many who call themselves Christians will not necessarily "go to church" at all—will not even identify themselves with a congregation or a specific denomination. Will the Church then reject these people or ignore them, simply because they refuse to take out exclusive membership cards in the religious club? This is certainly the present attitude of many clergymen with whom I have talked: "If a man doesn't go to church he is a bad Christian. . . . He is a member who enjoys the benefits but doesn't pay his dues. . . . Public worship is part of the duty of a Christian. . . . If everyone stayed away, the Church would eventually disappear. . . . How else can a man support the faith and learn the will of God?"

This attitude presupposes that churches must be confined to buildings, but in the New Age it is possible that such buildings may cease to exist or, at least, lose their importance. The day may be coming when, rather than the people flocking to the church, the church will have to flock to the people. John Lawrence, the editor of *Frontier,* writes that he finds it "impossible to believe that Asian or African Christians will not need to find radically new forms of worship and ministry when once we begin to take it seriously that the church does not exist for herself but for the world." [11] But why confine prophecy to the Asians and the Africans? Why not the Americans, Canadians, and British? It is highly likely that, in the Western world, we too need to find radically new forms for worship and ministry, and for very similar reasons—our world is changing as radically as the Asian and African worlds are changing.

To which the traditionalists will certainly cry out: "But what is left? You have banned the sermons, scrapped the pulpits, abandoned the familiar concept of God the Father, thrown out the Bible stories, and done away with religion. Now you want to tear down the churches or at least relegate them to side streets. What, in God's name, is left?"

What is left, in God's name, is what was there at the outset: Christian love, in all its flexibility, with all of its concern for real people rather than for any fixed set of rigid principles. This is the force that has been dissipated by "religion." Canon John Collins, of St. Paul's, London, has put the argument in far more eloquent terms than I can in his Passion Sunday sermon:

We of the churches so easily find ourselves judging the world and placing the world under God's condemnation. We blame those outside the churches for their secularism, for their worldliness, for their will to power, for their will to pleasure. We credit the non-church people with responsibility for the spread of materialism and for the lack of any peace in the world. But it is, under the Cross of Christ, we who have been privileged to see the true meaning of the Cross who are become blind. Having seen the realistic significance of the life and death of Jesus, and then having failed to allow its significance to play any realistic part in our everyday lives, we blindly stumble along the road which must lead to destruction.

The Church . . . rejects its own faith. For in rejecting the realistic significance in the affairs of men of the Cross of Christ, in rejecting the realism of the way of the Cross, in preferring the power of the sword to the power of love, it proclaims to the world that the death of Christ was, if not a total failure, if not the defeat of love, at best only the gesture of an unrealistic

dreamer, or the inevitable end of one who unwisely refused to
compromise with the powers that be. . . . We are guilty of
blasphemy. . . .

Canon Collins went on to say that no amount of ecclesiastical
reform could save a church that, by its non-commitment in the
world, had largely seemed to have abandoned its faith in the
power of love. The Church, he said, could be saved only by "a
determination to revolutionize society in such a way that it may
more easily and more willingly conform to the pattern of a society committed to the way of love."

But to revolutionize society, to get out into the world beyond
the Church, to act and if necessary to sacrifice, the Church must
revolutionize itself. Is this possible? In spite of those progressive
souls within the Church who believe that it has already entered
into the opening stages of a great reformation, I remain skeptical. The Church, in the words of one ex-minister I know, "is very
much in danger of dying from blood-letting. Because it doesn't
use its blood, because it hasn't got the normal healing qualities
that grow out of vigorous activities, it is liable to suffer a wound
from which it will slowly bleed to death, and no one will notice
its going when it finally expires. It will leave a residue, but its
impact will be virtually gone."

This is certainly a considerable possibility—that, though the
Church continues in its various forms for another thousand years,
building new structures, piling up new statistics, raising new and
larger funds to preserve its institutional entity, it will become
very much like the British Commonwealth, without power to
move or change or stir the hearts and souls of men.

"If there is a revolution, where will it come from?" I was asked
this question by a group of priests during one of the several discussions that accompanied the writing of this book, and I answered
without much thought, "Probably from the theological schools."
I gave this answer because in the secular world it is often the
students and their professors who spark a revolt. Having since
looked more deeply into the matter, I no longer believe it possible.
In Dr. C. R. Feilding's words: "The theological schools are well
behind in the revolution. Certainly the good schools have good

scholars on their staffs. But these people are all bound up with research in their specific fields. It's rather like a medical school where there are experts in everything except in what to do with the patient. . . ."

But there seem to be two ways in which a truly Christian reformation could come about. It could come about through some terrifying persecution of the Christian Church—a persecution that would rid the Church of those of little faith, of the status-seekers and respectability-hunters, of the deadwood who enjoy the club atmosphere, of the ecclesiastical hangers-on and the comfort-searchers. Once the Church becomes the most uncomfortable institution in the community, only those who really matter will stick with it. At this point, one would expect the Church to come back to those basic principles of love, faith, and hope that have made martyrs out of men

One would expect it but one cannot be sure; for in those countries where the Christian churches have suffered persecution, there is little evidence that they have been revitalized. The churches that continue to exist behind the Iron Curtain have yet to demonstrate that modern persecution produces modern martyrs, perhaps because the Communist persecution has been of a subtle nature.

In Russia, the churches have been more ignored than attacked; the doors have not been shut; but when one enters them one gets the feeling more of a home for senior citizens than a vital, living institution. Is it possible that the Church was so far gone in these countries before the revolution, so tied to the old social establishment, that all its vitality was sapped? One suspects as much. Still, it may be too early to tell yet whether the challenge has brought a Toynbeean response. The German Church certainly seemed to buckle under Hitler's Nazis in the Thirties. Yet that period served to produce a brilliant and courageous handful of philosopher-theologians who, as a result perhaps of their example and experience, are in the forefront of Christian radical thought today.

The chance of persecution in the Western world, short of a complete Communist takeover, is slight. It is not the established Church that stands in danger of persecution; it is those Christian radicals who question it and who are, in time-honoured fashion, attacked as heretics. But it is from the ranks of the so-called heretics that the revolution must surely come if it is to come at all.

If it does come, it is likely to come as the result of the actions of one man, of some spiritual genius, perhaps yet unborn, who will take all the incredible laws, postures, and myths of today's Church and turn them inside out, so they have some relevance in the New Age. Such a man, seeing through the murky varnish of wealth, snobbery, self-seeking, and apathy, which overlays the Church, to the essential message at its core, would by sacrifice and total commitment work his modern miracles.

He would have to be a man of vigour, humour, passion, concern, guts and, above all, action. It is fairly certain that he would not move with the elders of the Church but with its youth; it is probable that he would not mingle with the leaders of society but with the rejected; it is predictable that he would be a master of contemporary methods of communication, but that his real communication would be through his own commitment to his faith. It is axiomatic to say that he would be reviled as the most dangerous of heretics for slicing through the labyrinth of myth and dogma in which the Church is currently enmeshed; it is more than likely that, being an enemy of the establishment—religious, social, and political—he would be denounced as a traitor. And it is in the cards that society would find some modern means of crucifying him.

Ragged, cast out, abandoned, denied, and finally extinguished, he would seem to his contemporaries to have failed miserably in his obviously vain task. Yet there would be one or two who, at the moment of his death, would be moved to the point that they would commit their own lives to his ideals. It is possible to believe that this number might grow into the Christian Church of the New Age.

It does not follow that it will necessarily be called anything of the sort. It is possible that it may have a new name, incorporating the name of the man who sacrificed himself that it might flourish anew. But names are immaterial. Like titles and offices, vestments and priestly uniforms, ecclesiastical façades and human shells, they are important only to those who put more trust in outer garments than in the spirit within.

NOTES

PREFACE

[1] Mumford, Lewis, *Faith For Living* (New York: Harcourt, Brace and Company, 1940), p. 138.
[2] *Ibid.*, p. 140.
[3] *Ibid.*, p. 170.
[4] *Ibid.*, p. 166.

THE PAST / WHY I LEFT THE ANGLICAN CHURCH

[1] Bonhoeffer, Dietrich, *Letters and Papers from Prison* (London: SCM Press Ltd., 1953), p. 97.

ONE / THE ABDICATION OF LEADERSHIP

[1] Harrison, Tom, *Britain Revisited* (London: Victor Gollancz, Ltd., 1961), p. 54.
[2] *Ibid.*, p. 54.
[3] *Ibid.*, p. 54.
[4] Lynd, Robert S., and Helen Merrill, *Middletown, A Study in American Culture* (New York: Harcourt, Brace and Company, 1929), p. 317.
[5] Harrison, *op. cit.*, p. 56.
[6] Mumford, *op. cit.*, p. 163.

7 Henson, H. Hensley, *War-time Sermons* (London: Macmillan & Co. Ltd., 1915), Preface, vii; p. 69.

8 Mackinnon, Rev. A. G., *The Spirit That Wins* (Edinburgh: Oliphants, 1918).

9 Denney, James, *War and the Fear of God* (London: Hodder & Stoughton, 1916), p. 29.

10 Dudden, F. Holmes, *The Heroic Dead and Other Sermons* (London: Longmans, Green & Co., 1917), p. 129.

11 Yinger, J. Milton, *Religion, Society and the Individual* (New York: The Macmillan Co., 1957), p. 261.

12 Matthews, Shailer, *Patriotism and Religion* (New York: The Macmillan Co., 1918), p. 115.

13 Sneath, E. Hershey, editor, *Religion and the War* (New Haven: Yale University Press, 1918), p. 20.

14 Rihbany, Abraham Mitrie, *Militant America and Jesus Christ* (Boston: Houghton Mifflin Co., 1917), p. 10; p. 73.

15 Sneath, *op. cit.*, p. 93.

16 *Ibid.*, p. 93.

17 Haig, Douglas, *The Private Papers of Douglas Haig* (London: Eyre & Spottiswoode, 1952), p. 143.

18 Matthews, *op. cit.*, p. 17.

19 Sneath, *op. cit.*, p. 22.

20 Wolff, Leon, *In Flanders Fields* (New York: The Viking Press, 1958).

21 Tuchman, Barbara, *The Guns of August* (New York: The Macmillan Co., 1962).

22 Horne, Alistaire, *The Price of Glory* (London: The Macmillan Co., 1962).

23 Wright, Ronald Selby, editor, *Front Line Religion* (London: Hodder & Stoughton, 1941), p. 115.

24 *Ibid.*, p. 119.

25 *Ibid.*, p. 173.

26 Runbeck, Margaret Lee, *The Great Answer* (Boston: Houghton Mifflin Co., 1944), p. 170.

27 *Ibid.*, p. 175.

28 Crossman, R. H. S., *Esquire Magazine* (November 1963), "Apocalypse at Dresden."

29 *Toronto Daily Star*, August 13, 1945.

30 *The Telegram* (Toronto), August 13, 1945.

31 *The Globe & Mail* (Toronto), March 14, 1962.

32 Yinger, *op. cit.*, p. 258.

[33] Thrall, Charles A., and Herbert Blumberg, *Fellowship Magazine* (September 1, 1963), "Fellowship Survey on Attitudes of U.S. Clergy."

[34] *The Globe and Mail* (Toronto), February 17, 1964.

[35] *The Christian Century* (August 3, 1960).

[36] Myrdal, Gunnar, *An American Dilemma: The Negro Problem and Modern Democracy* (New York: Harper and Brothers, 1944).

[37] Allport, Gordon W., *The Nature of Prejudice* (New York: Doubleday Anchor Books, 1958), p. 417.

[38] Loescher, Frank S., *The Protestant Church and the Negro, A Pattern of Segregation* (New York: Association Press, 1948), p. 9.

[39] Moton, Robert R., *What the Negro Thinks* (New York: Doubleday, Doran, 1932), p. 253.

[40] Loescher, *op. cit.*, p. 106; p. 109.

[41] *Anglican Congress, 1963* (Toronto: The Anglican Book Centre, 1963), p. 106.

[42] *Ibid.*, p. 81.

[43] Loescher, *op. cit.*, p. 30.

[44] Myrdal, *op. cit.*, p. 563.

[45] Loescher, *op. cit.*, p. 50.

[46] Campbell, Ernest Q., and Thomas F. Pettigrew, *Christians in Racial Crisis, A Study of Little Rock's Ministry* (Washington: Public Affairs Press, 1959), p. 40.

[47] *Ibid.*, p. 40.

[48] *Ibid.*, p. 126.

[49] La Violette, Forrest, *Canadian Japanese and World War II* (Toronto: University of Toronto Press, 1948), p. 196.

[50] Gibbs, Mark, and T. Ralph Morton, *God's Frozen People* (London: Collins Fontana Books, 1964), pp. 54-5.

[51] Mumford, *op. cit.*, p. 162.

[52] Mitchell, Broadus and George S., *The Industrial Revolution in the South,* quoted in Myrdal, *op. cit.*, p. 869.

[53] Myrdal, *op. cit.*, p. 873.

[54] *United Church Observer* (May 1, 1961).

[55] *Maclean's Magazine* (May 18, 1963).

[56] Hollingshead, August B., *Elmtown's Youth* (New York: John Wiley & Sons, Inc., 1949), p. 260.

[57] *Ibid.*, p. 266.

[58] Greene, Gael, *Sex and the College Girl* (New York: The Dial Press, 1964).

[59] Edwards, David L., and John Robinson, editors, *The Honest To God Debate* (London: SCM Press, Ltd., 1963), p. 43.

⁶⁰ Heron, Alastair, editor, *Towards a Quaker View of Sex* (London: Friends Home Service Committee, 1963), pp. 10-71.

TWO / THE TYRANNY OF THE RELIGIOUS ESTABLISHMENT

¹ Kierkegaard, Sören, *Kierkegaard's Attack upon "Christendom"* (Princeton: Princeton University Press, 1946), translated by Walter Lowrie, p. 28.
² Adorno, T. W.; Else Frenkel-Brunswik; Daniel J. Levinson; R. Nevitt Sanford, *The Authoritarian Personality* (New York: John Wiley & Sons, Inc., 1964), p. 727.
³ Allen, Ralph, *Maclean's Magazine* (February 25, 1961), "The Hidden Failure of Our Churches."
⁴ Kierkegaard, *op. cit.*, p. 30.
⁵ Berger, Peter L., *The Noise of Solemn Assemblies* (New York: Doubleday, 1961), p. 9.
⁶ Quoted in Charles B. Templeton, *Evangelism for Tomorrow* (New York: Harper, 1957), p. 28.
⁷ Edwards, *op. cit.*, p. 268.
⁸ Mumford, *op. cit.*, p. 18.
⁹ Edwards, *op. cit.*, pp. 223-4.
¹⁰ Keene, Donald, *Living Japan* (New York: Doubleday, 1959), p. 89.
¹¹ Yinger, *op. cit.*, p. 311.
¹² Lynd, Robert S., and Helen Merrill Lynd, *Middletown in Transition, A Study of Cultural Conflicts* (New York: Harcourt Brace and Company, 1937), p. 372.
¹³ Herberg, Will, *Protestant—Catholic—Jew* (New York: Doubleday & Co. Inc., 1955), p. 88.
¹⁴ Allen, *op. cit.*
¹⁵ Yinger, *op. cit.*, p. 280.
¹⁶ Packard, Vance, *The Status Seekers* (New York: David McKay Company Inc., 1959), p. 196.
¹⁷ Anglican Congress, *op. cit.*, p. 79.
¹⁸ Fiss, James F., *The Religious Press in America* (New York: Holt Rinehart and Winston, 1963).
¹⁹ Berger, *op. cit.*, p. 43.
²⁰ Lynds, *Middletown, op. cit.*, p. 333.
²¹ *Ibid.*, p. 402.
²² Seeley, John R., R. Alexander Sim, Elizabeth W. Loosley, *Crestwood Heights* (Toronto: University of Toronto Press, 1956), p. 216.
²³ Warner, W. Lloyd, *et al.*, *Democracy in Jonesville* (New York: Harper & Brothers, 1949), p. 167.

[24] Seeley, *et al.*, *op. cit.*, p. 214.

[25] Hollingshead, *op. cit.*, p. 246.

[26] *Ibid.*, p. 257.

[27] Lynds, *Middletown in Transition*, *op. cit.*, p. 306.

[28] Hollingshead, *op. cit.*, p. 254.

[29] *Ibid.*, p. 252.

[30] *Ibid.*, p. 253.

[31] Warner *et al.*, *op. cit.*, p. 157.

[32] Lynds, *Middletown in Transition*, *op. cit.*, p. 306.

[33] Warner *et al.*, *op. cit.*, p. 153.

[34] Packard, *op. cit.*, pp. 196-202.

[35] *Ibid.*, p. 206.

[36] Pope, Liston, *The Annals of the American Academy of Political and Social Science* (March, 1948), "Religion and the Class Structure."

[37] Warner, W. Lloyd, and Paul S. Lunt, *The Social Life of a Modern Community*, pp. 356-9.

[38] Loescher, *op. cit.*, p. 81.

[39] Phillips, J. B., *The Church Under the Cross* (New York: The Macmillan Company, 1956), p. 47.

[40] Burchard, Waldo W., *American Sociological Review* (October, 1954), "Role Conflicts of Military Chaplains," reprinted in Yinger, *op. cit.*, p. 591.

[41] *Ibid.*, p. 593.

[42] *Ibid.*, pp. 595-8.

[43] Campbell and Pettigrew, *op. cit.*, pp. 121-6.

[44] *Ibid.*, pp. 107-8.

[45] Kierkegaard, *op. cit.*, p. 84.

[46] Allport, *op. cit.*, p. 424.

[47] *Ibid.*, p. 420.

[48] *Ibid.*, p. 421.

[49] *Ibid.*, p. 422.

[50] Adorno *et al.*, *op. cit.*, p. 219.

[51] *Ibid.*, p. 218.

[52] *Ibid.*, p. 221.

[53] *Ibid.*, p. 731.

[54] Rose, Peter I., *The Public and the Threat of War, Social Problems 11* (1963), pp. 62-77.

[55] Canadian Peace Research Institute, Box 70, Clarkson, Ontario; unpublished.

[56] Hollingshead, *op. cit.*, p. 245.

[57] *Ibid.*, p. 248.

58 Adorno *et al., op. cit.,* p. 730.
59 Loukes, Harold, *Teen Age Religion* (London: SCM Press Ltd., 1961).
60 Hollingshead, *op. cit.,* p. 110.
61 *Ibid.,* p. 118.
62 *Ibid.,* p. 117.
63 *Ibid.,* p. 391.
64 Berger, Peter L., *The Precarious Vision* (New York: Doubleday, 1961), p. 198.
65 Allport, *op. cit.,* p. 415.
66 Lynds, *Middletown in Transition, op. cit.,* p. 316.
67 *Ibid.,* p. 318.
68 Packard, *op. cit.,* p. 201.
69 Wakefield, Dan, "Slick Paper Christianity," reprinted in Stein, Maurice; Arthur J. Vidich; and David Manning White; editors; *Identity and Anxiety* (Glencoe: The Free Press, 1960), p. 412.

THREE / THE FAILURE OF COMMUNICATION

1 Quoted in Templeton, *op. cit.,* p. 22.
2 Berger, *The Precarious Vision, op. cit.,* p. 153.
3 Lamott, Willis Church, *Revolution in Missions* (New York: The Macmillan Co., 1954), p. 114.
4 Leyborn, James G., *The Christian Century* (August 31, 1960), "Idols We Bow Before."
5 *Anglican Congress, op. cit.,* pp. 99-100.
6 Edwards, *op. cit.,* p. 126.
7 Bonhoeffer, *op. cit.,* p. 147.
8 Edwards, *op. cit.,* p. 89.
9 *Ibid.,* p. 237.
10 Tillich, Paul, *The Eternal Now* (New York: Charles Scribner's Sons, 1963), p. 113.
11 *Anglican Congress, op. cit.,* p. 94.
12 Harrison, *op. cit.,* p. 56.
13 Lynds, *Middletown in Transition, op. cit.,* pp. 312-3.
14 Harrison, *op. cit.,* p. 62.
15 Lynds, *Middletown, op. cit.,* p. 372.
16 McLuhan, Marshall, *Understanding Media* (New York: McGraw-Hill, 1964).
17 *Toronto Daily Star,* April 4, 1964.
18 Robinson, *op. cit.,* p. 47.

[19] Edwards, *op. cit.*, p. 143.

[20] Robinson, *op. cit.*, p. 33.

[21] Pike, James A., *The Christian Century* (December 21, 1960), "Three-Pronged Synthesis."

[22] *Baptist News* (February 1964).

[23] *Toronto Daily Star*, March 24, 1964.

[24] Tillich, *The Shaking of the Foundations* (New York: Charles Scribner's Sons, 1948), p. 57.

[25] Bonhoeffer, *op. cit.*, p. 142.

[26] Adorno *et al.*, *op. cit.*, p. 221.

[27] Edwards, *op. cit.*, p. 267.

[28] Robinson, *op. cit.*, p. 132.

THE FUTURE / IS REVOLUTION POSSIBLE?

[1] Robinson, *op. cit.*, p. 126.

[2] Edwards, *op. cit.*, p. 186.

[3] *Ibid.*, p. 85.

[4] *Ibid.*, p. 47.

[5] Mumford, *op. cit.*, p. 159.

[6] Lynds, *Middletown in Transition*, *op. cit.*, p. 311.

[7] Adorno *et al.*, *op. cit.*, p. 739.

[8] Yinger, *op. cit.*, p. 270.

[9] Edwards, *op. cit.*, p. 271.

[10] Tillich, *op. cit.* p. 90.

[11] *Anglican Congress*, *op. cit.*, p. 90.